About Andrew Coulson and *Educational Freedom*

"Andrew Coulson was a brilliant man who devoted his life to studying and advancing freedom through school choice. Though no longer with us, his ideas will live on for generations through the researchers, advocates, and lawmakers who have embraced the philosophy that education simply works best when students and families are put in charge."

—Gov. Jeb Bush, Founder, President and Chairman of the Board of Directors of the Foundation for Excellence in Education

"When you think about the history and growth of parental school choice, it's hard not to think of the many icons of the movement, among them Milton Friedman, John Walton, the Gleason family, and Andrew Coulson. For years, Andrew Coulson was a key voice promoting markets in k-12 education, even when it wasn't popular. This book is a fitting tribute to his importance and his legacy."

—Robert Enlow, President and CEO, EdChoice

"Andrew Coulson was a rare phenomenon: A first-rate intellect who entered a debate with absolutely no prejudices, vested interests, or commitment other than to find the truth. For this reason alone, his ideas deserve serious consideration."

—Gene V. Glass, Emeritus Regents' Professor, Arizona State University

"In a field top-heavy with the smug and the strident, Andrew Coulson was education reform's best happy warrior. You'd be happy, too, if you were as gifted as Andrew at skewering arguments that leaned on political orthodoxy, philosophy, or preference, instead of cold, hard facts. We are infinitely poorer having lost Andrew so young. But we should count ourselves lucky that he left such a rich legacy—and so many disciples primed and eager to continue his important fight."

—Robert Pondiscio, Senior Fellow and Vice President for External Affairs, Fordham Institute

"Andrew Coulson was a giant in the field of education policy. The first education policy book I ever read was *Market Education: The Untold History,* and it left a lasting and profound impression on me, as it has with so many individuals who work on education choice and reform. This current volume not only reflects on Coulson's countless contributions to education policy, but considers his positions in the context of unfolding education policy debates, shedding light onto current and long-held debates ranging from the relative merits of vouchers versus tax credits to the best ways to measure education freedom itself. This collection of essays penned by scholars that continue to build on and magnify Coulson's work is a testament to the considerable influence he had, and the impact his ideas will continue to have in shaping education policy debates for decades to come."

—Lindsey Burke, Director, Education Policy Studies and Will Skillman Fellow in Education

"This book is chockablock with provocative ideas, powerful theories of human flourishing, agreeable disagreements, and fact-based reasoning. As such, it is a worthy tribute to the late, great Andrew Coulson."

—Patrick J. Wolf, Distinguished Professor, University of Arkansas

EDUCATIONAL FREEDOM

EDUCATIONAL FREEDOM

Remembering Andrew Coulson • Debating His Ideas

EDITED BY NEAL McCLUSKEY
AND JASON BEDRICK

CATO INSTITUTE
WASHINGTON, D.C.

Published by Cato Institute Press.

eISBN 978-1-944424-53-4 (digital)
ISBN 978-1-944424-52-7 (print)

Cover design by Jon Meyers.
www.cato.org

Contents

Introduction

Neal P. McCluskey and Jason Bedrick

Andrew Coulson's career in education policy, tragically ended by brain cancer in February 2016, was not long. Andrew was only 48 years old when he died, and his crusade to vastly improve education was his second calling. As you'll read in this volume, Andrew had been part of other groundbreaking work before entering the world of education policy. That success could easily have led a less driven, less caring person to rest on his accomplishments and retire early. Instead, he took on a new challenge. And while Andrew's years relentlessly pushing to transform moribund, government-dominated education were short, his impact was great. He packed a lifetime's worth of energy, and many decades worth of thought, into the all-too-limited time he had.

We both had the pleasure of working with Andrew—technically for Andrew, but it never felt that way—when he was the director of the Cato Institute's Center for Educational Freedom, and Neal worked with Andrew even before that. Indeed, Neal recalls the early days of a debate Andrew sparked in the early 2000s, when Neal was a neophyte policy analyst at the Center for Education Reform. Andrew was the most outspoken advocate in the country for delivering school choice through tax credits rather than vouchers, and his declarations of their superiority touched off friendly but spirited debate. In 2001, when he was a senior research associate at the Social Philosophy and Policy Center, Andrew released a Cato Policy Analysis making the case for tax credits, "Toward Market Education: Are Vouchers or Tax Credits the Better Path?"

Truth be told, in our early days, we both preferred vouchers to tax credits. Neal even said as much in his Cato job interview. He wanted credit- and deduction-free flat taxes, and what libertarian could disagree with that! But in the context of education policy, Andrew helped persuade Neal that scholarship tax credits were the better way to go.

Andrew got his start in education policy with his book *Market Education: The Unknown History*. As the title suggests, the book laid bare the history of education that many advocates for public schooling have not wanted us to hear. Previously, people such as leading progressive educator Ellwood Cubberley had written education histories that made it seem like humanity's evolution ebbed or flowed exclusively on the degree to which government supplied education. In contrast, *Market Education* showed readers that, historically, education did not require government provision. Indeed, people consumed abundant and much more effective education in times and places in which free people—not the government—controlled learning. Driving this message home—that leaving free people to work voluntarily with one another is the key to educational excellence—was at the core of everything Andrew did in education policy, including his work on tax credits, his examinations of educational productivity, his preschool education commentary, even his work on terrorism and madrassas.

Ultimately, Andrew worked to maximize human flourishing, and he knew that goal requires freedom in education. In the process, he either touched off, or contributed mightily to, lots of education policy debates. Despite Andrew's powers of persuasion, of course, many of those debates continue, but they do so greatly enriched by Andrew's contributions. In this book, several people who knew Andrew well—including some who sparred with him from time to time—reflect on those contributions and carry on some of those crucial debates.

In the first chapter, Bob Bowdon, founder of the indispensable website ChoiceMedia.tv, writes about Andrew's life, including the job Andrew had before diving into the ocean of education policy. Let's just say for the moment, Microsoft founder Bill Gates has taken a big personal—and financial—interest in education. Do we know who might have put a bug in his ear?

In the next chapter, former Cato Institute education analyst Adam Schaeffer offers a full-throated defense of scholarship tax credits, the school choice mechanism that Andrew most ardently championed. Then, George Clowes, senior fellow at the Heartland Institute, takes issue with Andrew's preference for credits over vouchers, continuing a friendly debate that has gone on for years. Following that, Jason Bedrick reconsiders Andrew's views on the constitutional and policy dangers of public funding as they pertain to the latest arrow in the school choice quiver, education savings accounts. Can this type of publicly funded account withstand legal challenges that vouchers could not? And might their design mitigate Andrew's concerns about the potential for public funds to bring harmful regulations?

Moving to the bigger picture, Jay Greene, head of the Department of Education Reform at the University of Arkansas, joins Jason in discussing Andrew's historical work, the work that put Andrew on the education policy map.

The last three chapters address Andrew's ultimate goal for school choice—a full, free market in education. The first of these is by James Tooley, professor of education policy at Newcastle University and author of the award-winning Cato book, *The Beautiful Tree: A Personal Journey into How the World's Poorest People Are Educating Themselves*. Years ago, Andrew became fascinated with James's accounts of his world travels and his discovery of abundant for-profit schools in many of the poorest parts of the globe. James's chapter discusses his findings, Andrew's friendship, and the need for free-market education throughout the world.

But how do we measure freedom in education? Trying to figure this out was a project that Andrew undertook with incredible zeal, eventually resulting in the Cato Education Market Index, a metric for scoring any education system according to the degree to which decisions were made centrally, or by individual parents and educators. John Merrifield, an economist at the University of Texas at San Antonio, was an adviser on the Market Index project, and he thinks there is a better way to measure the market orientation of a system: his own Education Freedom Index. Anyone desiring a better education system should engage in this debate.

In the last of the policy chapters, Neal McCluskey discusses what he considers the most important—but overlooked—reasons that school choice is essential: freedom of conscience, equality, and social harmony. Andrew recognized, and wrote repeatedly, that public schools—"democratically controlled" government schools—are inherently unequal, with majorities, or powerful minorities, deciding what every child will or will not be taught. But Andrew did not say that any choice solves the problem: vouchers, too, encroach on conscience rights. As Andrew argued, the best way to maximize freedom and educational equality while minimizing coercion is through tax credits.

The book concludes with a number of moving testimonials penned soon after Andrew's death by people who worked with, knew, or just knew *of* Andrew. This outpouring began within hours of Andrew's passing, and we are honored to be able to reproduce so many powerful memorials here.

Andrew Coulson may no longer be with us physically, but his ideas endure.

1. Getting to Know Andrew Coulson

Bob Bowdon

In 1994, a Microsoft software programmer with four and a half years on the job arranged a meeting with his manager. At the appointed time, without much small talk, Andrew Coulson offered a letter of resignation. Surprised, the manager asked why he was quitting. Equally surprising was Coulson's answer (as retold later by Andrew's wife, Kay). Andrew said to his boss, "I'm leaving because of you."

Many managers might gird themselves at such a moment, anticipating an unseemly string of critiques and complaints that could flow from the mouth of a departing employee suddenly free from the need to keep up appearances. But that was not about to happen. Instead, Andrew said, "I can see that you love your work. It brings you joy, fulfillment, and you just love what you do. I don't have that. I want to go find something that I love." Those who knew him can imagine the earnest, naked, forthright face he must have offered at that moment.

Microsoft didn't completely fail Andrew in the love department. Through that job, he met a young Cincinnati native named Kay Krewson, a Microsoft software tester who would become his wife. But just as he followed his heart with Kay, he wanted to follow his heart professionally.

It bears mentioning that in his resignation, Andrew didn't quit just any job. He quit The House that Bill Built, a company that arguably defined modern technology and business dominance of the era.

Many periods in American business are associated with one juggernaut company and its killer product. In the 1910s, it was Ford Motor Company and the Model T. In the 1960s, it was IBM and the System/360. In the first decade of the 21st century, perhaps it was Google and its search engine. But in the 1990s, that juggernaut company was undisputedly Microsoft, and its product was a little something called Windows. This was the professional rocket ship from which Andrew Coulson voluntarily disembarked. As a developer working on the famed Windows 95, Andrew was tossing away a job that millions of people would have clung to for dear life, for both the professional prestige and the potential financial windfall it could ultimately bestow. Looking back, however, those who knew him best understand his choice. Most rugged individualists with the gift of irrepressible optimism simply aren't cut out to be company men, and neither was this one.

In fact, the seeds of his next endeavor had already been planted. A few years earlier, Andrew had read with interest about a public referendum in neighboring Oregon to amend the state constitution. The ballot initiative called for interdistrict school choice, which would have let parents send their children across the imaginary political lines called "school districts," and it would have let families declare private school tuition costs as credits against taxes. "Clearly, that will pass," Andrew thought. "Slam dunk. Piece of cake. Put a fork in it." That was, until two-thirds of Oregon voters rejected the initiative.

The result puzzled him. Why on earth would Oregonians make the oxymoronic choice against choice? What could motivate people to get in their cars and drive to a polling place to stridently reject their right to make a decision—especially one affecting the lives of their children? The conundrum stayed with Andrew, and a few years later, the newly emancipated young programmer returned to this perplexing question—thus changing the course of his professional life.

Andrew Joseph Coulson was born May 4, 1967, in the Canadian province of Quebec, the fourth child of Violet and Donald Coulson. They were an iconoclastic family from the start, as native English speakers marooned in a French-speaking province. Despite the language barrier, it didn't take long for the neighbors to get to know Andrew. At either five or six years of age, he decided to offer a bouquet of flowers to his mom for Mothers' Day. Driven by both generosity and a young child's sense of creative problem solving, he promptly cut off the tops of flowers from yards all around the suburban neighborhood, assembled them to the best of his pint-sized ability, and presented the bounty to a delighted Mrs. Coulson. After thanking her son, she was immediately curious about his source of the raw material, as most mothers might be. The revelation led to a multistop floral apology tour that the neighbors understandably found charming.

Andrew's high school years involved French horn during the school year and sailing in the summertime on the lakes of Quebec. And while anyone hoping to be accepted at the highly competitive McGill University as a math major needs absolutely superb grades, older brother Stuart says that Andrew was much more than a good student during his adolescence. He was always curious, always cheerful, and always good company.

Presumably, if your eyes are moving across these words, you already know that Andrew Coulson very much did fulfill the quest he laid out during his Microsoft resignation: to find professional work that he loved. By 1999, he had published his landmark book, *Market Education: The Unknown History*. It examined education through the ages and across continents and found that when families spend their own money on schooling, just as with everything else, they get better results than when someone else spends money on their behalf. The volume was hailed by no less than Nobel Prize–winner Milton Friedman as an "unusually well written and thoroughly researched book."

Market Education was potent enough to get the attention of the Mackinac Center for Public Policy, which eventually hired Andrew as their senior fellow in education policy. He was good enough, in fact, that they hired him without requiring him to move to Michigan. A few years later, the Cato Institute hired him as director of the institute's Center for Educational Freedom. Again, he was good enough that they hired him without requiring him to move to Cato's Washington, D.C., home.

To begin to understand Andrew Coulson, however, is also to understand his irreverent, absurdist, and playful sense of humor. How many think tank analysts went to see the 2002 movie *Jackass* not once, not twice, but three times in the theater (accompanied by their wives, no less)? Andrew did. What other nationally respected policy experts developed a hobby of detonating plastic bottles, an activity that Andrew's friend John Nesby called "the glue that bonded our relationship"? Nesby, a professional chef and neighbor of the Coulsons, said, "We would shoot BB guns; we would light firecrackers off. Then we would get a little bit more extreme. We used to make dry ice bombs out of plastic bottles, dry ice, and water, and then we'd shoot them with pellet guns and make big explosions. It was just an absolute riot for a couple of grown men to be running around in the woods after a hard day's work, with a glass of chardonnay or a craft beer in hand and blowing stuff up."

In 2014, a 47-year-old Andrew Coulson worked out in the gym above the garage one day and afterward came out to talk to Kay. He told her that he got a weird taste and smell in his mouth. The sensation was strange enough that he thought he should tell her about it, in case it turned out to be something important. After a couple of days, he got the weird taste and smell again. Then it started to happen more frequently. Within four weeks of the first sensation, he began to get headaches, severe enough that he would lie in bed, unable to work despite continuous dosages of Tylenol.

First, the doctor said it was allergies and suggested he treat his symptoms with nasal sprays. When he went back to the doctor, the diagnosis switched to sinus infection, and he was prescribed antibiotics. Soon the pain was bad enough that he started vomiting. Kay took him to an emergency room where they did a CAT scan. That led to the next wrong theory—a brain infection—and a prescription for an MRI at a different facility. Only then did the correct diagnosis finally emerge, a grade 4 glioblastoma. Andrew, with his wife by his side, was told that the life expectancy for a person with his type of brain tumor is 15 months. The news of a terminal prognosis came about six weeks after the first symptom, during a regular treadmill workout.

Many people, no matter what stage in life, would be understandably depressed by the ominous news. But this man was not. You can talk to Andrew's widow, brother, and close friends. You can ask his professional colleagues. And if you knew him, you can review your own correspondences with him over the course of 2015. There's simply no account of futility or bitterness or nihilism. There's not even a coarsening or no-more-time-for-bullshit toughness. Andrew Coulson, as the end neared, stayed funny.

Also absent were grand gestures and end-of-life reconciliations. Andrew and Kay did talk about going back to Hawaii "one last time," but there was no discussion of a bucket list. Such late-hour recalibrations, it seems, aren't necessary for the people already leading the life they want.

Even his last few months of Facebook entries reveal an irrepressible spirit. The majority of the posts don't pertain to his illness. In one, he expressed relief that he'd learned which brand of yogurt had become the official yogurt of the National Football League. In late December, when Hillary Clinton extemporaneously said that she, "Wouldn't Keep Any School Open That Wasn't Doing A Better Than Average Job," Andrew, with about six weeks to live, summoned the strength to post, "Garrison Keillor please call your office."

The posts that referred to his illness were also spirited. On December 17, 2015, he wrote, "Just had my 37 millionth blood draw and saw a sticker on a table that suggests cancer patients aren't the only ones who get 'em. . . . It read 'Alleged Father.'"

Two days later, Andrew had a stroke. A few days after that, he posted, "Brain tumors being so 2014 I decided to try on a stroke for size. Definitely new and different. For the time being immobilized on my left side."

This was the Andrew Coulson that resonated with countless people who met and knew him. Thomas Shull, his colleague at Mackinac, might have summed it up best when he wrote in a blog post, "There was no one I enjoyed working with more than Andrew—a sentiment I suspect all his friends and coworkers share. . . . He was a good man, and he will be missed by virtually everyone who knew him."

While most of us don't like to think about it much, we'll all have to leave this world someday, perhaps before we think it's our time, perhaps without finishing everything that we're working on, and perhaps leaving loved ones who'll miss us dearly. When that day comes, may we all say goodbye with as much grace as Andrew Joseph Coulson.

2. Tax Credit–Funded Choice: Reform for "Transformationists"

Adam B. Schaeffer

Great scholars tend to have a few things in common: they tend to be inordinately productive, creative, and influential with those who follow them in their field. Andrew Coulson was all of those things and much more.

Coulson contributed to our understanding of education systems and policy in many ways, but I think his greatest contribution was his development of a comprehensive argument for the superiority of tax credits for funding educational choice and achieving the goals of the school choice movement. He promoted education tax credits because he kept in mind the most important factors in building a real, sustainable market for education: (1) locating financial responsibility at the source of the funds; (2) avoiding and overcoming legal challenges; (3) avoiding market-killing regulations; and (4) ensuring positive, short- and long-term political dynamics.

I should make an explicit note here about the purpose of this chapter. There are, very broadly speaking, two kinds of education reformers—those who seek the total transformation of the education system and "tweakers." Coulson was in no way the latter. He was not one to spend his time considering minor adjustments to the current system. Transforming a massive industry, one woven into the fabric of our nation and its politics, is not an easy task, and it will not be accomplished without many small steps along the way. But the goal of choice advocates such as Coulson and myself has always been a broad and deep shift in how the education system functions. This chapter is written for those who want to transform the system, not tweak it. It is a review of the reasons a "transformationist" should greatly prefer the use of tax credits, rather than government money, to fund educational choice.

My first introduction to Andrew Coulson came when I was in graduate school, in 2004. I'd written an article for National Review Online on vouchers. Using a recent *West Wing* episode as a lead-in, I argued that conservatives and Republicans should use school choice as a wedge issue among Democrats, pushing targeted vouchers to woo minority voters. Someone working in the choice movement wrote to compliment me on the article but gently suggested I might be missing some important concerns about school choice policy. He attached a late draft of a paper Coulson had written for the Mackinac Center: "Forging Consensus."[1] I read it, and that was it. In terms of practical impact, principle, public opinion, politics, regulations, and legal barriers, he made a thoroughly convincing case for consensus on what the goal of school choice proponents should be.

Coulson's work directly inspired my PhD dissertation, examining how school choice messages and policies interact, and I ultimately went to work for him at the Cato Institute. It is no exaggeration to say that everything I have written on education reform since then has been a recapitulation or extension of Coulson's thinking and analysis.

Much has changed since that seminal paper was published, but the case Coulson laid out holds up remarkably well. Indeed, much of the evidence has grown stronger in support of education tax credits over vouchers or government-funded education savings accounts (ESAs) as a mechanism to fund choice in education and ultimately build a dynamic market in K–12 education.

A key point to keep in mind regarding Coulson's work is this: he believed the goal of the school choice movement should be to build a robust, dynamic education market. The goal should not be to help just low-income kids, or children with disabilities, because the children who need help the most will be best served by a free-market education system that continually adapts and improves. A large, free, dynamic market with a wide range of choices will improve educational and life outcomes for all children, most of all those most in need.

Coulson laid out much of the rationale for his vision of the ideal educational system in his seminal book, *Market Education: The Unknown History*.[2] In the book, he made his case not just deductively from libertarian first principles, but inductively, from a review of the history of educational systems and theories that was surprisingly broad and deep at the same time. Following *Market Education*, Coulson spent years making the case for education tax credits as the best policy mechanism for establishing a true market in education.

Recently, ESAs have become very popular. The idea is to establish savings accounts and use the money deposited in those accounts—

and the funds that accrue over time—on education expenses. The funding mechanism has become associated almost exclusively with direct government payments into the ESAs. This approach has much to recommend it, but the advantages of using tax credits to fund school choice remain. The source of and mechanism for funding education is of great importance, for both short- and long-term outcomes.[3]

In the remainder of this chapter, I will review the key aspects of the case for supporting school choice directly with funding from individual taxpayers rather than with government money.

Overview of Education Tax Credits

Education tax credits reduce the amount a taxpayer owes the government for each dollar spent on a child's education or scholarships for children who need them. For instance, if a business owes the state $4,000 in taxes and donates $4,000 for scholarships, it will pay $0.00 in taxes and can choose the organization that receives the donation. In some programs, the credit is less than 100 percent, but in all cases the mechanism can be thought of as a waiver of a tax obligation—the taxpayer gets to keep more of her own money to spend on education. This funding mechanism can, of course, be used to fund ESAs instead of, or in addition to, scholarships. Tax credits for donations to scholarship organizations can help support school choice for lower-income families, and personal-use credits can help middle-class families.

Donation tax credits have been the most popular credit policy. In these programs, any charitable organization can file to become a Scholarship Granting Organization (SGO). SGOs receive tax credit donations from businesses or individuals and then give scholarships to children to attend private school. Here again, this funding mechanism can be used to fill ESAs.

Financial Responsibility

In "Forging Consensus," Coulson argued that "across the centuries and around the world, direct financial responsibility for parents is associated with significantly better student outcomes and school conditions, with keeping costs more firmly under control, and with the minimization of fraud."[4] In supporting these claims, Coulson marshaled modern and historical examples, from ancient Greece to 19th-century Britain and America, to modern India.

Evidence abounds that parental financial responsibility is important, and most people know intuitively that people tend to be much more thoughtful and careful in spending their own money than that of others. Ultimately, service providers are most concerned about pleasing those who pay them. Parental choice isn't the only consideration—how the system is funded matters as well.

Nonrefundable, personal-use tax credits (in other words, money that a family actually earned and owed in taxes) are the only mechanism that gives parents full, direct financial responsibility. As Coulson noted in "Forging Consensus," parental financial responsibility "is the only means by which parents have historically managed to retain control over what, where, and by whom their children are taught. Without financial responsibility, parental choice has sooner or later been lost. Third-party payment in elementary and secondary education has consistently been associated with eventual third-party control over the content and delivery of that education."[5]

Donation tax credits involve third-party funding of educational choice, but the people or entity that earned the money direct the donation of the funds. In other words, oversight, accountability, and diversity are built into the funding mechanism. A diversity of taxpayers and SGOs act as a bulwark against market-killing centralization and control.

Legal Considerations

Courts do not consider tax credits to be government money, whereas vouchers are considered government money.[6] This distinction means that vouchers face much greater legal peril than do tax credits. Six state courts have ruled that because parents, not the government, spend the government dollars, vouchers do not conflict with the state constitution. Three other state courts—Vermont, Colorado, and Florida—have found that voucher programs use government funds in ways that do violate state constitutional restrictions and have therefore struck them down or limited their use to secular private schools. The Arizona Supreme Court struck down the state's voucher program, but later upheld its publicly funded ESA.

While the use of government funds does not automatically cause vouchers to run afoul of state constitutional restrictions, it does open myriad avenues of attack to which nonrefundable tax credits are not vulnerable. As Supreme Court Justice Anthony Kennedy explained in a ruling that upheld an education tax credit program, "a dissenter whose tax dollars are 'extracted and spent' knows that he has in some small measure been made to contribute to an establishment in violation of conscience. . . . [By contrast,] awarding some citizens a tax credit allows other citizens to retain control over their own funds in accordance with their own consciences."[7]

State courts have repeatedly ruled that vouchers are government funds.[8] The disbursement of government funds to religious schools is expressly prohibited in most states by turn-of-the-century anti-Catholic "Blaine" amendments that were meant to keep public funding in Protestant-influenced public schools and away from Catholic parochial schools. Many states also have what are called "compelled support" clauses, which get the same result through different language, precluding any citizen from being compelled to support religious institutions or activities through their taxes. These religious provisions are the highest profile threats to voucher programs, but vouchers are vulnerable to many other common state constitutional clauses regarding education.

Some defeats in court have been based on seemingly innocuous education clauses common in state constitutions. For example, in Florida, the court struck down vouchers on the basis of a clause mandating a "uniform" system of education. That ruling had nothing to do with religion, but it was possible because vouchers are considered government funds.[9]

Furthermore, the degree to which a controversial policy is perceived to be subject to legal jeopardy—regardless of legal precedent specific to the issue—has been shown to dampen consideration by legislatures in the first place.[10] Politicians and other political actors consider the disposition of the courts and are much less likely to fight for and pass controversial legislation that has a high probability of being voided by the courts. Survey data show that "state legislators admit they write laws in anticipation of responses from the state supreme court," and statistical evidence derived from actual legislative activity supports the conclusion that policymakers respond to "perceived threats or opportunities shaped by the ideological complexion of state supreme courts."[11] The general legal difficulties that vouchers face, in other words, can significantly dampen political and legislative support for them.

The fact that the courts and the public regard vouchers as government funds and tax credits as private funds has a number of important consequences. It means that tax credits are less likely to be challenged in court, less likely to be overturned by a court, less likely to come with burdensome regulations, and less likely to accumulate regulations over time. The most important implication is this: tax credits are a viable option in many states where effective voucher programs are likely to be struck down on state constitutional grounds. And even where government funds are directed to ESAs, the source of the funding can still cause legal and political troubles.[12]

Regulation

The fact that tax credits, unlike vouchers and government-funded ESAs, are not government-funded is important in other ways, too. School choice opponents have a more politically and legally compelling case for imposing burdensome regulations on voucher-redeeming schools and the use of ESA funds than they do for schools and ESAs that benefit only indirectly from tax credit programs.

In a government-funded system, the decision on whether or not to continue funding students at any particular school is made by government actors through the political and legal process, not by individuals through market interactions within civil society. Marginal, controversial cases tend to drive public demand for more restrictive or prescriptive rules; many people who pay the taxes that fund the school will demand that their money not be used for a purpose they oppose. Over time, such regulations, added in response to periodic difficulties, accumulate until little freedom remains for education service providers.

Indeed, research supports the conclusion that government funds tend to bring a higher regulatory burden to education, at least in regard to vouchers.[13] Even ESAs should not be considered immune from regulatory creep when funded directly by the government. The Supplemental Nutrition Assistance Program (SNAP), commonly known as "food stamps," for instance, is essentially a "food savings account" funded by the government. And the government has assembled an intricate web of restrictions and a formula determining what can and cannot be purchased with SNAP funds.

For example, beer and wine, despite having food value, cannot be purchased with SNAP funds. Candy and cookies are allowed. The government has decided that pumpkins are allowed, as they are edible; "however, inedible gourds and pumpkins that are used solely for ornamental purposes are not eligible items." Gift baskets are allowed, but not "if the value of the non-food items exceeds 50 percent of the purchase price." That rule goes for "items such as birthday and other special occasion cakes"—they're good to go "as long as the value of non-edible decorations does not exceed 50 percent of the purchase price of the cake." It's not clear how one determines the value of non-edible items in a gift basket or on a birthday cake, but surely there is a complicated formula somewhere on the Department of Agriculture website.[14] Beyond this complicated web of restrictions, there are always calls for more—even drug testing of the recipients.[15]

The use of government funds always compels taxpayers to support the actions taken by recipients, even if only in a very small way. It implicates them in others' behavior and choices, forcing individuals to engage the political process to coerce an outcome. In contrast, tax credits allow the free exchange of funds and services within civil society and an education market without the need for coercion. Either the funds are spent directly by the taxpayer who earned them or given freely by the taxpayer who earned them to a person who needs them.

Political Dynamics

Funding school choice through tax credits has one massive additional advantage over direct government funding—political dynamics. School choice policy advocates often underestimate this consideration. Using tax credits to fund educational choice is generally more popular with the public, easier to defend in public debate, easier to enact into law, and easier to defend and expand after passage.

Education tax credits tend to be more popular than vouchers, and vouchers are much more vulnerable to claims that government funds are being diverted to some citizens to the detriment of others. A 2016 public opinion survey by the journal *Education Next*, for instance, found that low-income-targeted tax credits garner 53 percent support and just 29 percent opposition—a positive 24-point margin of support. Low-income-targeted vouchers, in contrast, have a negative 11-point margin of opposition (37 percent for and 48 percent against).[16]

The lower support for and greater opposition to vouchers seems to be driven to a significant degree by the use of government money to fund private school choice. The word "voucher" is not mentioned in the survey; rather, the question refers to the government "helping to pay the tuition" at a private school—a description that could just as easily describe a government-funded ESA. The survey also used a second version of the voucher question and found significant erosion in the balance of support when it described vouchers as a policy that will "use government funds to pay the tuition." With that language, support fell to just 31 percent and opposition rose to 55 percent—a negative 24-point margin of opposition to using government money to fund private school choice.

Tax credits tend to be quite popular in general, much more so than direct government spending. Americans are familiar with and well disposed toward tax credits, a common policy vehicle. The Hope Scholarship tax credit and child tax credits, for instance, are widely recognized and popular tax breaks. Various kinds of college tax credits regularly garner over 80 percent support.[17]

Some critics have lamented the proliferation of special interest tax credits and deductions, but they proliferate for a reason. Tax credits are a popular and relatively easy way to encourage spending on particular kinds of activities. Credits for education expenses have the same advantages.

Tax credits are not just more popular and resistant to attack than vouchers. Unlike programs funded with government money, tax credit–funded choice programs actually build a network of institutions and individuals with the resources and interest to defend and expand the credits. Because individual taxpayers direct their money to the kind of education they want to support, they become invested in their chosen school or organization. A woman who takes advantage of a tax credit benefits both directly and personally from the policy, even if she doesn't use the tax credit for her own child, because she can enjoy spending her money on a child or educational mission she supports. In a similar fashion, businesses that claim tax credits on donations benefit from and have a stake in the law.

Perhaps most important, tax credits create a new and permanent institutional support system for choice. The SGOs that arise to administer the donation tax credits form a new and powerful block of political interests that do not exist under a voucher or government-funded ESA program. SGOs have already proven effective advocates for the defense and expansion of choice programs in Arizona, Florida, Georgia, and Pennsylvania. These organizations can quickly disseminate information to and mobilize parents, businesses, and schools, and they have the funds and financial interests to do so.

In Pennsylvania, for instance, scholarship organizations funded through the donation tax credit program have become a serious political force. They act as an institutional base for supporters and beneficiaries, translating this constituency into a mobilized political force. Andrew LeFevre, former executive director of the REACH Alliance, a Pennsylvania school choice organization, described the role of his organization and that of the scholarship organizations in the state:

> Upon passage of the [Educational Improvement Tax Credit] EITC program in 2001, REACH made a strategic decision to work on helping to set up a scholarship organization (SO) in as many of the 67 counties as possible in order to begin the process of connecting the people involved with the program—most importantly the parents and children—with their elected officials. As we enter the 2007–08 school year, there are now approximately 180 SOs (as well as over 300 [educational improvement organizations] EIOs and 80 Pre-K SOs) that have been created all across the Commonwealth. These groups serve as a vital link between the families that they serve and the legislators that have been responsible for more than doubling the program cap over the past six years.
>
> REACH works with the participating SOs to help them better understand the importance of maintaining that personal relationship with their elected officials and the media to show the tremendous positive impact that the program has on children and families in their local districts. Many SOs now require their families who receive scholarships to write to their elected officials to thank them for their support of the program, generating thousands of letters a year to Harrisburg on behalf of the EITC program.[18]

Tax credits, in other words, create interest groups with a direct stake in defending and expanding the program. In turn, scholarship organizations use their resources to overcome collective action problems and mobilize individuals who benefit from the program.[19] Voucher and government-funded ESA programs do not create these connective institutions and thereby leave program beneficiaries and supporters with a more difficult organizational task.

Despite partisan polarization on the program when it was first passed, in 2011 the Pennsylvania House voted to more than double the size of the education tax credit program, with 96 percent in favor and only 4 percent opposed. Indeed, in a year when a government-funded school voucher policy failed, the funding for education tax credits in Pennsylvania was increased by 100 percent. In 2010, a major expansion of Florida's education tax credit program passed both houses overwhelmingly, with support from 42 percent of Democrats and 52 percent of the legislative black caucus.[20] (Nearly every Republican voted yes.) The program received just one Democratic vote when it was created in 2001. New or expanded tax credit initiatives were signed by Democratic governors in Arizona, Iowa, and Pennsylvania in 2006. That same year, a Democrat-controlled legislature in Rhode Island passed a donation tax credit. And the Democratic governor and legislature in Iowa raised their tax credit dollar cap by 50 percent in 2007.

Everyone who participates in a tax credit program—individuals, businesses, and scholarship organizations—has personally invested in the program and has a strong, direct interest in defending and expanding it. Vouchers and government-funded ESAs simply do not create that kind of communitywide, direct, and personal investment because the government decides how and where to allocate collective funds.

Government-funded choice programs create a dispersed, uncoordinated constituency, composed primarily of low-income families. Tax credit–funded programs create a coordinated network of organizations and individuals with the resources and drive to force lawmakers to attend to their concerns. In the medium and long term, these differences in political dynamics are critical for achieving a broad, robust, dynamic market in education.

Conclusion

Tax credit–funded school choice is superior to government-funded choice in terms of encouraging and preserving parental financial responsibility, avoiding and overcoming legal challenges, avoiding market-killing regulations, and short- and long-term political dynamics.

Government-funded private school choice in other countries and in the United States comes with and accretes many regulations. Regulations are much less of a concern with tax credits, which both the courts and the public view as private funds. For the same reason, education tax credits are much better in principle than government-funded school choice: tax credits allow the people who earned the money to disburse it to the kind of education they deem appropriate. Government-funded choice policies still compel taxpayers to support, say, a religious school when they are atheist, or a secular school when they are religious—even if only in some small way.

The difference between government-funded choice and education tax credits is the difference between welfare and charity. It's the difference between a government-funded, single-payer health insurance program and a combination of donation-funded health savings accounts and individual tax benefits for health spending. Tax credits preserve some accountability to, and allow for discretion by, the people who actually earned the money in the first place while still ensuring that all children have access to a wide range of good educational options.

These issues are all related to one another. Government funding of educational choice courts more legal problems and compels support of education to which many taxpayers will object. Because of that compulsion, people will demand restrictions on the use of their tax dollars. And because of those demands, the government will increasingly restrict and regulate how the education money can be used. The absence of freedom of choice for the taxpayer will naturally lead to a restriction of choice for the students using the money and the schools accepting the money. Education tax credits eliminate or greatly mitigate all of these concerns and problems with government-funded choice.

In addition to mitigating problems with government-funded choice, tax credit choice programs build a robust network of individuals and institutions that can mobilize support and expand the program over the long term. Government-funded choice policy cannot accomplish that result.

If we are to develop a true market in education and transform educational opportunities for all children, we need to think strategically and deeply about how each small step we take will promote or hinder the expansion of educational freedom in the long run. Government schools currently educate about 90 percent of all students, and the number of private schools educating the rest is too small to constitute a real market. The task ahead of us is to carve out and develop a market in education, a task that will take decades even with the best policies enacted.

Although government and credit-derived funds will both accomplish the same immediate goal of sending some children to an existing private school, only tax credit–funded programs provide a chance to transform the educational system in the long term.

3. Tax Credits Can't Create a Competitive Education Marketplace

George A. Clowes

I would like to acknowledge the contribution of Andrew Coulson to my development of a comprehensive menu of school choice options. It was Coulson's persistence in defending his views that prompted me to find ways of addressing the issues he raised and defending them against his challenges.

Andrew Coulson and I agreed on a central point: What is needed to improve the present K–12 system of public schools is the creation of a vigorous education marketplace, with different types of schools and education providers actively competing for students and their tuition dollars. Our differences lay in how to do it. His approach was to focus school choice reform efforts almost exclusively on the use of personal and scholarship tax credits, with the use of vouchers considered only as a fallback position in situations in which tax credits would not work. My position was, and still is, to focus reform efforts primarily on universal vouchers while also supporting a range of other school choice options because different parents and different education vendors need different school choice vehicles for a variety of valid reasons. We exchanged views in 2004, when he published the report "Forging Consensus,"[1] which argued for the superiority of tax credits. I responded with "Still No Consensus on School Choice."[2] We again exchanged our different views in 2008[3] at a conference on the design of school choice programs, held at the Clemson Institute for the Study of Capitalism.[4]

"Education markets have consistently done a better job than state monopolies of serving both our individual needs and our communal goals," declared Coulson 15 years ago. "Yet all market-inspired education reforms are not intrinsically or uniformly effective. They can succeed only to the extent that they support the conditions for a thriving education market and ensure that all families have access to that market."[5]

Drawing from his own research,[6] in which he examined modern and historical precedents, Coulson concluded that the conditions necessary for the effective operation of an education market are these:

- Parental choice of school
- Direct parental financial responsibility
- Freedom for educators to establish different types of schools
- Competition among educators
- The profit motive for educators
- Universal access

First, he argued, parental choice keeps schools focused on offering what parents value and helps avoid social conflicts over the content of instruction. Second, having parents pay some or all of the cost of their child's education is the only way, historically, that parental authority and school autonomy have been maintained. Third, like other free market operators, educators must be free to specialize; to innovate; and to set their own curricula, teaching methods, prices, and admissions policies. Fourth, there must be vigorous competition among schools, which would come from having a large number and variety of competing schools and large numbers of participating students. Fifth, for-profit schools must be included because they have an incentive to expand in response to excess demand for their services, unlike their nonprofit counterparts. Finally, some form of third-party financial assistance is required to ensure that low-income families have access to the education marketplace.

Coulson compared voucher and tax credit programs with regard to how well they met the necessary conditions for market education and how well they allowed all families to participate in that market. He concluded that tax credits are the better alternative. Not only are they easier to enact and defend, he argued, but also, "They are more effective at putting into place the freedoms and incentives necessary to the effective operation of the market, offer greater resistance to new regulation, decrease the risk of fraud and corruption, and avoid problems that might arise from state funding of religious schools."[7] He went on to recommend that "the school choice movement's single most important goal should be the establishment of an optimal Universal Education Tax Credit program, and, if that proves impossible, an optimal voucher program."[8] Subsequently, he advocated strongly for tax credits over vouchers.

My approach was to review the design features necessary for school choice programs to create a competitive education marketplace and thus be capable of reforming the public schools. I concluded that only universal vouchers could achieve this objective. While all school choice programs could rescue children from failing schools, only universal vouchers could reform the system because only they had the potential to achieve the levels of funding, participation, and direct competition necessary for such a marketplace to develop. I also concluded that it is better to provide parents with a variety of school choice options to choose from, with different programs serving different purposes and needs.[9] To that end, I proposed a comprehensive range of choices for parents and, equally important, a range of mechanisms to enable public, private secular, and religious schools to respond to competition. These choices involved a variety of public and private school options, including open enrollment, charter schools, vouchers, individual tax credits, and tax credit scholarships.

Because both proposals—Coulson's tax credit proposal and my full-menu school choice proposal—are intended to produce a competitive K–12 education marketplace, let us examine what conditions are necessary for the emergence of such a "thriving education market," as Coulson termed it.

Creation of a Thriving Education Market

A free and universally accessible market in K–12 education exists when a parent, as the consumer, has access to the funds necessary to buy a satisfactory package of educational services for his or her child from the offerings of a variety of schools and instructional service companies. The competing vendors would offer a range of goods and services of different prices, qualities, capabilities, and technological novelty. Vendors would compete for each parent's funds, and the ones best at securing them would have a strong incentive to expand. In such a market, no vendor would receive a preferential government subsidy or be subject to onerous regulation, and it would be relatively easy for new vendors to enter the market. Low barriers to entry encourage vendors to operate efficiently and keep parents happy or else risk loss of business to new startups.

The American public schools system is far from this ideal. Most decisions regarding the allocation of taxpayer funds to schools are made by state and local government officials rather than by parents.

In addition, the schools are government-owned, government-run, government-staffed, and government-monitored.

In 1955, Milton Friedman suggested a different approach. Although government financing of K–12 education was appropriate, he argued that government-run schools were not justifiable in a predominantly free enterprise society because the freedom of the individual, or the family, is the objective of such a society, not "an indiscriminate extension of governmental responsibility."[10] To elevate parental freedom within the existing school finance system, he proposed that a subsidy, in the form of a school voucher, be made available to all parents regardless of which school they attended. He predicted that this system would result in the emergence of "a wide variety of schools" that would compete and produce greater effectiveness and efficiency over time.

Friedman's proposal attracted little public attention until, some three decades later, concerns about the quality of public schools had become widespread. By 1989, Albert Shanker, president of the American Federation of Teachers, was warning his members that if public schools did not improve soon, then "policymakers are going to find a cure that will be radical and painful," such as using public funds in private schools.[11]

"We need system-wide change," wrote Shanker, because the system is the problem. "It's time to admit," he wrote, "that public education operates like a planned economy, a bureaucratic system in which everybody's role is spelled out in advance and there are few incentives for innovation and productivity. It's no surprise that our school system doesn't improve; it more resembles the communist economy than our own market economy."[12]

Shanker's warning came too late. The "radical and painful" cure he warned about—using public funds in private schools—was already being enacted in Wisconsin, with the creation of a voucher program that targeted children from low-income families in Milwaukee and featured vouchers that could be used as full tuition at a participating secular private school.

Vouchers are a powerful school reform tool because they shift the funding from being institution centered to being child centered. With vouchers, charter schools, and open district school enrollment policies, public education funding follows the child to the school chosen by his or her parents; vouchers empower parents over school boards and school principals because if the parents are not satisfied with the education the schools provide for their child, they will take their child—and the child's education dollars—somewhere else.

Tax credits are another tool to enhance school choice, but they take a significantly different approach from vouchers. Rather than reallocating the government's education funding, tax credits instead encourage private citizens and corporations to donate to nonprofit scholarship organizations that help families pay private school tuition, or reduce the taxes paid by parents and legal guardians who pay for tuition and other educational expenses.

The key feature of tax credits is that they would prompt new spending on K–12 education outside of and in addition to the current system. Vouchers, on the other hand, would redirect current education dollars to schools chosen by parents.

What Does a Competitive Market in K–12 Education Look Like?

Would we recognize a competitive market in K–12 education if we saw one? As initial criteria for such an assessment, we have Coulson's six requirements that I detailed above. To these, we can add requirements that other school choice advocates have identified as important, and we can specify conditions that have proven critical to the competitiveness—or lack thereof—of various voucher programs.

For example, most school choice advocates expect a competitive education market to produce quality improvements and cost savings from innovation and experimentation. However, Friedman pointed out that this outcome requires the inclusion of higher-income families in school choice programs because they are the early adopters of new developments and innovations.[13] Economist John Merrifield has also identified the stability of the program as a key element of an education market, because producers need to have confidence in the reliability of a projected revenue stream.[14]

In a 2008 study of why voucher programs had not produced the vibrant education market that reformers had expected, I concluded that voucher programs had to include three design features to produce the level of competition necessary to spur improvements in the public schools.[15]

First, the voucher value must be substantial. A voucher value capped at half of the district schools' annual per-pupil allocation or less reduces competition by limiting the number and kinds of private schools that are willing to participate. This, in turn, limits the number of students who can participate.

Second, the money must truly follow the child. Schools will respond to competitive pressure only if there are financial consequences when students leave. Private schools must actively compete for students. However, when voucher programs or state education policies include "hold harmless" provisions or otherwise insulate districts from the financial consequences of decreasing enrollment, schools in those districts have little incentive to respond competitively.[16] For vouchers to work, the rule of "the money follows the child" must be applied to rejected schools as well as to chosen schools.

Third, voucher competition must be explicit. The response of district schools to competition from vouchers depends on the proximity and size of the competitive threat. When faced by a well-publicized,[17] imminent, and specific threat from vouchers, district schools respond strongly to the competitive challenge. However, when faced with a small and diffuse competitive challenge from vouchers, district schools respond only weakly.

Combining these added requirements with Coulson's, our final list of requirements for a competitive education market is as follows:

- Parental choice of school
- Direct parental financial responsibility
- Freedom for educators to establish different types of schools
- Explicit competition among educators
- The profit motive for educators (and the need for a reliable revenue stream)
- Universal access (including low- and high-income families)
- Per-pupil funding comparable to the public schools, with the funding following the child

An indication of what are the critical elements among those requirements comes from a surprising place: charter schools. This is surprising because such schools have not been highly regarded by many free market advocates, including myself; they have been viewed as compromised tools for reform because they are subject to significantly more state regulation than private schools that accept vouchers. Market entry is severely restricted; charter schools may not have a religious affiliation; parents cannot be required to contribute financially to tuition; and limitations are placed on parental choice, educator freedom, and enrollment boundaries. In addition, per-pupil funding is only 72 percent of that in a traditional district school, on average.[18]

However, as Lisa Snell pointed out more than a decade ago, "charter schools have met more of the criteria of a free market in education than most current tax credit and school voucher programs."[19] First, she noted, charter schools have added substantial new school capacity since the first one opened in 1991; by February 2016, more than 6,800 charter schools were serving nearly 3 million children nationwide at a cost of almost $21 billion a year, according to data from the Center for Education Reform.[20] Second, said Snell, numerous for-profit providers—for example, White Hat Management and National Heritage Academies—have developed successful school models, branded them, and set about replicating them.

Although charter schools are public schools, for-profit companies may be involved in operating them. Two-thirds of charter schools are independently run, nonprofit, single-site schools; another 20 percent are run by nonprofit organizations with multiple sites; and 13 percent are run by for-profit companies with multiple sites.[21] According to a 2011–12 study, the largest of the for-profit companies were Imagine Schools (operating 89 schools), Academica (76), National Heritage Academies (68), K12 Inc. (57), and Edison Learning (53).[22] The largest charter school operator is KIPP (Knowledge Is Power Program), a nonprofit that established a successful model and now has 200 schools in 20 states serving nearly 80,000 students.[23] Although charter school approaches and specializations vary widely—such as performing arts, foreign language immersion, and project-based learning—the top six focuses are college prep (30 percent); core knowledge (16 percent); science, technology, engineering, and math (STEM) (8 percent); blended learning (6 percent); and constructivist and back-to-basics (both at 5 percent).[24] The creation of all these new schools recalls Friedman's prediction that vouchers—in this case, public school vouchers—would result in the emergence of "a wide variety of schools."

What accounts for the success of charter schools in not only promoting competition between schools but also in persuading entrepreneurs to invest hundreds of millions of dollars in the creation of almost 7,000 new schools since 1991? I have already detailed the limitations placed on charter schools that deter competition, but what are the features that appear to have been critical to their success in enhancing competition? First, they offer universal access—all students are eligible. Second, competition is explicit because charter school enrollment gains and district school student losses are usually well covered by the news media. Third, the money follows the child and traditional district schools generally face financial consequences when they lose students. Fourth, per-student funding, while not generous, is adequate, and it comes from a reliable and predictable source.

We now have a set of requirements for the creation of a competitive education market, plus a good indication of the factors that are critical to the success of that process. Let us now examine tax credits in light of those findings.

The Education Marketplace with Tax Credits

If tax credits are going to create an education marketplace, the place to look for any signs of that would be in Florida, where the state's 15-year-old tax credit scholarship program provides one of the highest per-pupil scholarship values relative to district school spending.

According to EdChoice (formerly the Friedman Foundation),[25] the Florida tax credit scholarship program was expected to provide scholarships of about $5,680 to more than 92,000 participants in 2016–17, or 3.3 percent of the state's 2,778,914 K–12 district school students in 2015–16.[26] The average scholarship is 85 percent of the state's average $6,681 elementary private school tuition and 64 percent of the state's average $8,926 private high school tuition.[27] The average scholarship value in 2014–15 was about $5,000,[28] which was 49 percent of the total expenditures per pupil of $10,156 for the state's district schools.[29] The program was close to its cap of $559.1 million, or 2 percent of the $27.9 billion in total state, local, and federal expenditures for K–12 education for 2014–15.[30] The cap increases by 25 percent each year when the credits claimed reach 90 percent of the cap, and with increased funding, the per-student funding cap on scholarships can also grow.

Although one of Coulson's objectives in using scholarship tax credits is to create a vigorous education marketplace with strong participation by for-profit operators, a breakdown of schools taking in the Florida scholarship tax credit shows that objective is far from being achieved. As of February 2016, of the 1,594 participating schools, 69 percent were religious and 31 percent were secular; of the 79,719 participating students, 82 percent attended religious schools and 18 percent attended secular schools.[31] In addition, the current list of schools does not indicate the participation of any secular multisite operators. With only a modest scholarship value, Florida's tax credit scholarship program—while extremely successful in many respects—has not attracted for-profit (or even nonprofit) entrepreneurs who might want to serve scholarship students the same way that charter school students are served.

Religious schools also predominate as recipients of tuition funds generated by Arizona's scholarship tax credit program, which is the nation's oldest, having started in 1997.[32] In 2014–15, the program served 30,049 children,[33] or just 2.7 percent of the state's 1,117,905 K–12 district and charter school students.[34] The average scholarship value was $1,846, or 21 percent of the state's 2014–15 total expenditures of $8,854 per pupil in district and charter schools.[35] A newer corporate tax credit scholarship for low-income children served 16,573 children in 2014–15 with a similar scholarship value of $1,892.[36] With such low scholarship values, it is highly unlikely that either of these programs would attract the interest of educational entrepreneurs.

Although tax credit scholarships may not spur the creation of new schools, their predominant use in religious schools not only supports the desire of many parents to provide a religious education to their children, it also illustrates the need for such scholarships in states with a large charter school presence. That's because charter schools draw students not only from public schools but also from private schools, and particularly from religious schools. A recent study[37] showed that in both New York and Michigan, roughly one out of every three charter-school students came from a Catholic school, a result supported by a Cato Institute study.[38] Tax credit scholarships play a vitally important role in providing the funds necessary for religious and other private schools to respond effectively to this competition from charter schools.

No Competition for Money

One explanation for why tax credits have not spurred the creation of a competitive marketplace is that the private schools involved do not compete directly for money with the district schools. Although the money from tax credits follows the child to the chosen school, that money is not derived from current K–12 education dollars but from a new source of funding. And while it is true that a continuing migration of district school students to private schools would ultimately result in a reduction of total funding for the district school, the district school may not be fully aware that it is losing students because of a school choice program. And that would tend to mute any competitive response by district schools. This intrinsic feature of tax credits—not competing directly for money with the public schools—limits the likelihood that tax credits would produce a vigorous education marketplace.

In the 2014–15 school year, total expenditures for U.S. K–12 district schools were $662 billion, or just over $13,300 per enrolled pupil, with 49.7 million students.[39] Using the charter school experience, we can expect that a taxpayer-funded voucher worth $10,000, or about 75 percent of district school spending, would be adequate to educate a student and to attract the interest of for-profit education vendors. However, to provide comparable-value scholarships funded by tax credits would require a very substantial increase in charitable donations. For example, providing a scholarship of $10,000 for just one in five district school students would require tax credit donations of almost $100 billion a year. Total charitable donations to education in 2015 were only $56 billion. To satisfy the funding requirements of tax credit scholarships with three-quarter price scholarships would require a huge increase in giving to education. If we use district school enrollment to scale up the $559.1 million Florida Tax Credit Scholarship Program to the national level, the program would be raising an estimated $10 billion a year for education, enough to provide scholarships worth $5,000 to only about 2 million of the nation's roughly 56 million school-aged children. While that is a significant achievement, it is not sufficient to create the kind of education market that Coulson envisioned.

Preserving Direct Parental Responsibility

Coulson also argued that tax credits were superior to vouchers because "tax credits do a better job of preserving direct parental financial responsibility."[40] That is certainly true for personal tax credits. But the problem with them is that the amount of the credit is too small to be of much benefit to most taxpayers because their income tax liability is small compared with the cost of an education at a private school. Thus, most parents would need to rely on an ample supply of tax credit–funded scholarships to send their children to private schools. That would still be the case even if credits could be applied to school property taxes, as an analysis below will show.

To ensure more active parental interest and direct parental responsibility with tax credit–funded scholarship awards, Coulson argued it would be beneficial for tax credit–funded scholarships to have a copayment. In fact, this is already the case with almost all current programs because the scholarship amount usually does not cover the full cost of private school tuition and must be "topped up" by parents. However, copayments or topping-up capabilities are also viewed as desirable design features of voucher programs. Current voucher programs that permit parents to top up voucher payments include Indiana's Choice Scholarship Program and Florida's McKay Scholarship Program for students with special needs, among others.[41]

Thus, for tax credit–funded scholarships as they are structured at present, parents almost always do have to use their own money to pay for the education of their child, which would meet Coulson's objective of preserving direct parental financial responsibility. However, because voucher programs also could—and frequently do—allow parents to supplement or top up voucher payments to meet the actual cost of private school tuition, his argument in favor of tax credits turns out not to be as strong as it appears initially. Indeed, given a choice between the two, it is not at all clear why parents should prefer a scholarship funded by tax credits over a voucher funded by taxpayers. Both are funded by "other people's money," both might need to be supplemented with money from parents, and both achieve the objective of paying for a child to attend a private school.

Even without a required copayment, vouchers and scholarships can still be structured to encourage parents to treat the other people's money involved as if it were their own. As Friedman famously pointed out, when people spend their own money on themselves, they seek the best value at the least cost, but when people spend other people's money on themselves, they seek the best value with little concern for the cost. However, under a 2002 voucher plan proposed by the Heartland Institute,[42] parents are incentivized to get the best cost–benefit from their voucher funds by allowing them to keep any voucher funds left over after paying tuition, place the money into an education savings account (ESA), and then spend the surplus funds on college tuition or supplementary tutoring services.[43] Although Coulson hailed the proposal as innovative, he concluded it was unlikely to achieve its stated goals because it still involved other people's money.[44] However, when a 2011 Arizona voucher program was built around the ESA feature with more flexible usage options, Heartland's view of the ESA's cost-control potential began to prevail.

"[T]wo features of ESAs—the ability of parents to completely customize their child's education and save for future educational expenses—make them distinct from and improvements upon traditional school vouchers," wrote Jason Bedrick and Lindsey Burke in 2015. "ESAs empower parents with the ability to maximize the value their children get from their education services. *And because they control how and when the money is spent, parents also have a greater incentive to control costs.*"[45] (emphasis added)

Giving parents the authority to decide when and where to spend other people's money does create a strong incentive for them to use the money cost-effectively. Although it's not the kind of direct parental financial responsibility that Coulson envisaged, it achieves the same objective.

Tax Credits Do Not Use Public Money

Coulson posited that the second most significant advantage of tax credit programs over vouchers is that they avoid the use of public money.[46] In *Kotterman v. Killian* (1999), the Arizona Supreme Court ruled that the state's education tax credits do not involve government spending but simply let taxpayers keep more of their own money. Therefore, donating the amount of the credit to a religious or secular scholarship-granting organization does not involve the use of public money. The state court decision was appealed to the U.S. Supreme Court, which refused to hear the appeal and thus let the lower court ruling stand. Subsequently, the U.S. Supreme Court reached the same conclusion in *Arizona Christian School Tuition Organization v. Winn* (2011), and several other state supreme courts have also held that tax credits—like tax deductions or tax exemptions—are not public money. To date, tax credit scholarships have a 100 percent record of being upheld as constitutional.

According to Coulson, the fact that tax credits do not use public money gives them two distinct advantages over vouchers with regard to (1) church–state entanglement and (2) regulation. Because all of the money involved in tax credit programs is the taxpayer's own and not the state's, there is no church–state entanglement issue and no necessity for public oversight and state regulation of the spending. I will discuss these two issues in turn.

The Issue of Church–State Entanglement

In *Zelman v. Simmons-Harris* (2002), the U.S. Supreme Court ruled that the Cleveland voucher program, which includes religious schools, does not violate the U.S. Constitution because it is not the state but parents who choose to spend voucher funds at religious or secular schools. However, Coulson points out that the constitutional issues regarding vouchers are less clear at the state level, where 19 states have prohibitions on the "compelled support" of religious activities that are contrary to the dictates of conscience. In addition, 36 states have a so-called Blaine Amendment in their constitution that forbids state funding of religious institutions or practices. These amendments were adopted as part of a bigoted 19th-century campaign to bar Catholic schools from receiving the same kind of government funding that was provided to the pervasively Protestant "common" schools of the time.

Coulson argued that because all but three states have a compelled support clause or a Blaine Amendment in their constitution, vouchers are much more likely than tax credits to run afoul of these state constitutional provisions. Future voucher litigation, he predicted, "will inevitably pit Free Exercise against Free Exercise. The question will be: does the free exercise right of parents (who want to use vouchers for religious schooling) trump the free exercise right of taxpayers (who object on moral or religious grounds to paying for that schooling). Because the U.S. Constitution does not provide clear guidance on how to resolve this conflict, the Supreme Court may well defer to state constitutional provisions that forbid compelled support of religion or state funding of devotional instruction."[47]

However, Coulson's remedy of abandoning vouchers in favor of tax credits is not an appropriate solution for two reasons. First, it gives credence to a false representation of vouchers—voiced most commonly by opponents—that modern voucher programs violate freedom of conscience by "compelling" taxpayers to provide direct aid to religious institutions and thus support religion with tax dollars. In fact, modern voucher programs involve aid to families, with the funds paid directly to parents who then freely choose to spend those funds at the religious or secular school of their choice. Even Robert Chanin, chief counsel for the National Education Association, admitted before the U.S. Supreme Court in 2002 that such a transfer of funds "was constitutional" because the intervention of parents breaks the circuit between school and state.[48]

Second, the remedy treats Blaine amendments as if they were acceptable tools for opponents to deploy in their attempts to strike down voucher programs. They are not. Efforts should continue to educate the public about the bigoted history of these anti-Catholic constitutional provisions and the need for their repeal. In the ruling on *Mitchell v.*

Helms (2000), U.S. Supreme Court Justice Clarence Thomas made clear that the high court viewed Blaine amendments as ripe for repeal:

> [H]ostility to aid to pervasively sectarian schools has a shameful pedigree that we do not hesitate to disavow. . . . [N]othing in the Establishment Clause requires the exclusion of pervasively sectarian schools from otherwise permissible aid programs, and other doctrines of this Court bar it. This doctrine, born of bigotry, should be buried now.[49]

In a 2009 Institute for Justice analysis of state constitution religion clauses, Richard D. Komer concluded that compelled support clauses should not present a barrier to school choice programs because only Vermont had used its clause to bar religious schools from a voucher program.[50] The situation with Blaine amendments is mixed because some states have used the amendment to bar items such as transportation and textbook benefits for students at religious schools. Komer suggests it "would be wise" to consider tax credit programs rather than vouchers in such states and to pursue vouchers and tax credits in the other states. This suggestion strikes me as a better strategy than abandoning vouchers, although my own preference would be to pursue vouchers in all Blaine Amendment states, with ultimate resolution by the U.S. Supreme Court.

The Issue of Regulation

Some advocates fear that school choice programs will bring a heavy regulatory burden to private schools that could stifle the emergence of market forces. There is no constitutional barrier to such regulation. In *Pierce v. Society of Sisters* (1925), a unanimous U.S. Supreme Court ruled that, although the "child is not the mere creature of the state," the state nevertheless has the power to regulate all schools, public or private, and that the government can establish rules and regulations for private schools even if the schools do not make use of public money.

Coulson argued that vouchers bring a greater risk of regulatory encroachment because they involve the use of public money. Tax credits do not use public funds and thus are much less likely than vouchers to bring additional government regulation to private schools. Many tax credit advocates do not support refundable tax credits because they involve government money, just like vouchers.

"Because of the greater resistance to regulation that follows from the absence of state funding under tax-credit programs, those programs do a better job of protecting all the criteria for effective markets from regulatory encroachment," declared Coulson.[51] The findings from several studies provide strong support for his view. After conducting a statistical analysis of 20 voucher and tax credit programs, Coulson concluded in a 2010 Cato Institute report that, while vouchers "impose a substantial and statistically significant additional regulatory burden on participating private schools," tax credits do not.[52] A 2014 study by Andrew D. Catt for the Friedman Foundation analyzed 23 school choice programs and found that the regulatory impact scores of private school vouchers were more than three times more negative than the scores of tax credit scholarship programs. In particular, Catt found that voucher programs have more regulations related to paperwork and reporting than tax credit scholarship programs do.[53] A 2013 study by David A. Stuit and Sy Doan for the Thomas B. Fordham Institute examined 13 school choice programs and also found that tax credit scholarship programs are "significantly less subject to additional regulations than voucher programs."[54] In 2015, the American Enterprise Institute (AEI) published an extensive survey of 954 private school leaders in three states with school choice programs. The survey found that existing and possible future regulations were top concerns among leaders of schools participating in the choice programs (and even more so for those who chose not to participate). Moreover, these concerns were higher in Indiana and Louisiana (which have voucher programs) than in Florida (which has a tax credit program). Also, although nearly 100 percent of schools participating in the voucher programs cited concerns with the paperwork and reporting burden involved, only about half of Florida participants cited this as a concern with the tax credit program.[55]

In the Fordham Institute study, the researchers conducted a survey of 241 participating and nonparticipating private schools in five cities with voucher programs to determine which kinds of regulation cause the most difficulty for private schools. They found that more than half of private school leaders said it was very/extremely important to be able to uphold admissions criteria, but only a quarter regarded having to take state tests or teach state curricula as very/extremely important.[56] More than 40 percent of respondents regarded these additional regulations as very/extremely important: allowing students to opt out of religious activities, the amount of paperwork required, and the maximum dollar amount of the voucher. Overall, the study showed that the more regulations a program had, the less likely schools were to participate. Even so, only 3 percent of nonparticipating schools cited their unwillingness to comply with program rules as the single most important reason for not participating. The most cited reason for not participating was low demand resulting from the lack of voucher-eligible families in the area.

The AEI study came to somewhat different conclusions regarding regulations and testing, possibly because the Fordham Institute survey focused on urban areas while the AEI study was statewide. The AEI researchers found that, far from being unconcerned about rules, nonparticipants cited their top-ranked concerns as possible future regulations and their effect on a school's independence and character. Also considered highly problematic by participants and nonparticipants alike were related concerns such as school autonomy, state curricular requirements, and requirements to take state tests rather than nationally normed tests.

The survey responses led the authors of the AEI study to offer a number of policy recommendations, which included increasing the voucher/scholarship amount and removing certain eligibility restrictions. These two recommendations mesh with the top two responses that the Fordham Institute study obtained from nonparticipating schools asked what regulatory changes would influence them to participate: expanding eligibility to all families and raising the maximum voucher amount. While a low-value voucher may be acceptable as reduced price tuition to fill empty seats in existing schools, the Fordham Institute researchers point out that it is unlikely to provide an incentive to add new seats or for new schools to open. "The current funding levels of most programs are insufficient to attract new school operators," Stuit and Doan noted, "in part because there is such strong competing demand for new schools in the charter school sector, where per-pupil funding is closer to that of traditional public schools."[57]

From these studies, we can conclude that Coulson was right: voucher programs do attract significantly more regulatory encroachment than tax credits do. However, different kinds of regulation represent different levels of encroachment. For example, a testing requirement is much more onerous when it mandates taking state tests rather than choosing among numerous nationally normed tests. The two regulatory changes that would do most to increase participation, and hence competition, are these: make access universal and increase the value of the voucher. These are key features of charter schools, which currently are sucking all of the oxygen out of the school choice marketplace.

There will always be pressure for more regulation than is necessary. As Thomas Jefferson observed, "The natural progress of things is for liberty to yield, and government to gain ground." One way to help guard against such encroachment would be legislation to preserve the autonomy of private schools and protect them against the imposition of any undue burden from additional regulation.

Reliability and Sufficiency of Funding Stream

Can tax credits provide the reliability and sufficiency of funding that is required to bring entrepreneurs into the K–12 education market? A 2001 Heartland Institute study of two proposed income tax credits for New Jersey estimated that the combined effect of the two credits—one to mitigate tuition costs and the other to encourage donations to scholarship organizations—would be to prompt 7 percent of public school students to transfer to private schools, increasing private school enrollment by about 40 percent.[58] However, the study also revealed a serious limitation of tax credits that are applied to state income taxes: the relatively small number of children that benefit. The tuition tax credit benefits only a small number of children because most families pay much less in state income tax than the cost of tuition at private schools. Even when the rules governing use of the tuition tax credits were relaxed, this produced only a few additional transfers of students out of the public schools.[59]

In addition, the study estimated the proposed scholarship tax credit was unlikely to raise sufficient funds to pay the full cost of tuition for all children who want to attend a private school. Although the scholarship tax credit could raise as much as a half billion dollars a year for scholarships in New Jersey, that amount was just 3.2 percent of the $15.6 billion a year spent on K–12 education by New Jersey state and local governments at the time the study was conducted.[60]

The actual experience of Florida's corporate tax credit program shows that the New Jersey estimates could be somewhat low. As previously noted, the Florida program provides scholarships averaging $5,680 to over 92,000 participants, or 3.3 percent of the state's K–12 district and charter school students. The program currently is capped at $559.1 million, or 2 percent of the state's total expenditures on K–12 education. The cap may be stepped up in 25 percent increments to a theoretical maximum of about $3 billion in state corporate income and insurance premium tax receipts. However, for a variety of reasons such as economic fluctuations and diminishing returns with smaller donors, a practical maximum of about $2 billion appears more likely, or about 7.5 percent of Florida's total spending on K–12 education. With a future scholarship amount estimated at $6,000 per student, a $2 billion fund could serve about 333,000 students, which is slightly less than the 360,000 students currently attending private schools in Florida and about 12 percent of the students attending public schools in 2015–16. This amount would provide the program with considerable room for growth in the near term but with a need for additional funding sources within a decade or so. To summarize, the Florida program currently is about half the size projected for the New Jersey program and could potentially grow to almost twice the size.

The Florida program has a small effect on competition, according to a 2011 study of the program by Northwestern University researchers David Figlio and Cassandra Hart. They found that the competitive effect of the scholarships produces a modest improvement in test scores for both scholarship students and public school students.[61] However, the situation in Florida could not be called a thriving education market for a number of reasons. First, as noted, the continuing predominance of religious schools in the mix of participating schools indicates that for-profit schools have little interest in this market. Second, while the scholarship value may be sufficient to fill empty seats, it may not be enough to incentivize the addition of new seats. Third, the scholarship value is unlikely to be increased significantly because the desire to help as many children as possible tends to lower the average scholarship value. Fourth, investors may have some concerns about putting capital at risk and relying on charitable donations for revenues.

Despite these limitations, tax credit scholarships are still an important school choice option. They have significant value in that they enable religious and secular private schools to respond to the competitive pressures imposed on them by charter schools—alternatives to traditional public schools that are attractive to private school parents because they offer free tuition and universal access. Pushing for tax credit scholarships should be a high priority for school choice advocates, including proponents of vouchers and charter schools.

To provide access to much larger tax liabilities, Coulson and his colleague Adam Schaeffer proposed applying the credit to property taxes as well as income taxes.[62] Yet even when property taxes are included, the tuition tax credit often falls short as a way for individual taxpayers to cover the cost of tuition at a private school. For example, after adding property taxes to the proposed New Jersey tuition tax credit discussed earlier, Coulson concluded that "even a combined property and income tax credit would leave many families with insufficient resources to cover all their private school expenses."[63] That finding is significant because if individual tax credits do not generate sufficient funds in New Jersey—where property taxes make up an unusually large proportion (almost two-thirds) of K–12 education resources—they certainly cannot generate sufficient funds in other states, where property taxes play a smaller role in education funding.

Thus, a school choice plan involving nonrefundable tax credits would need a scholarship component to provide funds not only for low-income families to exercise school choice but also for higher-income families whose combined state and property tax liability would still be insufficient to cover the cost of tuition at a private school. Schaeffer argued that his plan, with no cap on total contributions from property taxes, would generate substantial scholarship funds. Taxpayers could zero out the property tax payments they make to their local schools and redirect those funds to private schools and to private school scholarship organizations.

The operation of the plan was illustrated by describing an upper-income family, the Garcias, who donate 100 percent of the family's combined income tax, sales tax, and property tax liability for the year —$22,000—to three private school scholarship organizations. These organizations then fund scholarships worth up to 80 percent of current per-pupil spending in the public schools. To keep costs down and to encourage direct financial responsibility, the plan phases out benefits with increasing family income. Thus, while high-income families would be free to donate all of their substantial tax liability to scholarship organizations to benefit other children, they would not be able to use the tuition tax credit to benefit their own children nor receive any scholarships. With their $200,000 income, the Garcias would still have to pay the full tuition cost for the private school education they had chosen for their daughter Isabel.

Part of Milton Friedman's argument for universal vouchers was that high-income families need to be included in school choice programs—as beneficiaries as well as donors—in order to provide the necessary funding for innovation and experimentation. By reducing benefits for middle-income families and barring benefits for high-income families like the Garcias, Schaeffer's tax credit plan falls short of establishing the conditions necessary to create a competitive market. Access would not be universal and only low-income families would receive the high-value scholarships that would attract for-profit school operators.

It appears, then, that even if expanded to include property taxes, tax credits are unlikely to be as widely available or well funded as would be necessary to create a competitive marketplace. Nevertheless, Schaeffer's proposal for using property taxes to fund school choice programs is worth pursuing for vouchers as well as for tax credits. Creating a personal property tax credit for education is readily justified on fairness grounds. Parents who are paying to place their children in a local private school—thereby enriching the diversity of their community—should not be forced to also pay property taxes for their local public schools. Handling such a credit as an exemption, like homeowner and senior citizen exemptions, would be a relatively easy way for local government units to handle such a credit.

The Way Forward

Three requirements appear critical for the creation of a competitive market in K–12 education: universal access, a well-funded voucher or scholarship, and assurance that the money follows the child. Any school choice program that lacks these three components may rescue children from failing schools or help parents keep their child at a private school, but it will not create any significant competition in the education marketplace. To date, only charter schools have come close to having all three components, with both vouchers and tax credits severely limited by low voucher/scholarship amounts and restrictions on student eligibility.

Also, clearly, no one school choice program satisfies all the criteria that various reformers consider important for the issues they champion, nor is there one school choice program that is capable of satisfying the different priorities of parents and the range of concerns of taxpayers. After arguing back and forth with Coulson regarding the relative merits of different school choice programs, I examined what features are necessary for school choice programs to create the kind of competitive education marketplace that would reform the public schools. I came to the following conclusion:

> Just as one size does not fit all in public schooling, one size does not fit all in school choice. Parents need a variety of options to choose from, and it is not necessary to address the needs of all parents and children with a single school choice program. If different programs were designed to serve different purposes, parents would have a menu of educational options to choose from for their children.[64]

I developed a comprehensive proposal "to provide just such a menu that offers parents a full range of educational choices."[65] Only two of the options—charter schools and vouchers—have the funding adequacy and reliability to accommodate the inclusion of for-profit operators interested in expanding a model school beyond a successful single-site operation. But a wide variety of different single-site schools would provide competition among education providers and a wide range of choices for parents.

The proposed options, which have been refined since their original presentation, provide a range of choices to parents and, equally important, a range of mechanisms to enable public, private secular, and religious schools to respond to competition:

- Public school choice—interdistrict open enrollment and charter schools to provide the public school equivalent of vouchers
- Private school choice—lightly regulated school vouchers worth at least 75 percent of total per-pupil district school spending (with the ability to "top up" tuition) that parents could use at secular and religious private schools, including new all-voucher schools
- Education savings account[66]—for all children, worth at least 75 percent of per-pupil district school spending, redeemable for any approved educational services or products
- Special education voucher—based on Florida's McKay Scholarship voucher, which is fully funded and redeemable at secular and religious schools
- Individual income tax credit for educational expenses—to support parents' efforts to send their children to private schools
- Individual property tax credit for owners and renters[67]—for tuition at private schools or donations to a private school or to a child's tuition expenses

- Scholarship income tax credit for individuals and corporations—for donations to organizations directing scholarships to private schools

If we can agree that it is better for parents to have several different school choice options available for educating their child, we can also perhaps break down the artificial barriers that have emerged between advocates of the different school choice approaches. What is needed is for these "islands of school choice" to begin to communicate more with each other with the aim of supporting each other's proposals instead of remaining on the sidelines as observers or stepping forward as public critics. For example, when charter school advocates propose expansion legislation and want support from other school choice proponents, they would be more likely to get it if they would also advocate and support parallel legislation for tax credits so that private schools and particularly religious schools could better compete with them in an expansion environment. Voucher proposals in particular could use more support because they attract, and must deflect, much opposition criticism that is often applicable to other parts of the school choice movement, too.

Such mutual support would be very helpful, and it would not only help vouchers. As Jay P. Greene, professor at the University of Arkansas, wrote a few years ago with regard to teacher unions trying to strangle charter schools with red tape, "Vouchers made the world safe for charters by drawing union fire." But, he warned, when the unions have the voucher threat under control, "charters are in trouble."[68]

What is needed in each state is an informal coalition of school choice advocates who can regularly share information about new initiatives and problem areas to monitor. This would hopefully lead to a more supportive strategy among school choice advocates when legislative changes or initiatives are being considered.

Rather than promoting only one school choice option, school choice advocates should recognize that each approach has strengths and weaknesses. Tax credits are valuable in situations in which religious schools cannot participate in voucher programs, whereas vouchers have the best odds of meeting most of the requirements for creating a competitive marketplace for education. Embracing this more inclusive approach to expanding educational choice and providing mutual support across program boundaries would do much to advance the common cause of improving U.S. K–12 education.

4. Giving Credit Where Credits Are Due: Revisiting the Voucher vs. Tax Credit Debate

Jason Bedrick

Andrew J. Coulson burst onto the education policy scene in 1999 with the publication of his seminal book, *Market Education: The Unknown History*. A former software engineer for Microsoft, he soon rose to prominence as perhaps the foremost advocate for expanding educational freedom through tax credits. When *Market Education* hit the shelves, Arizona was the only state with a scholarship tax credit program. Since then, 16 more states have adopted similar policies. As of the 2015–16 academic year, nearly 220,000 students nationwide were using tax credit scholarships to attend the schools their families chose—considerably more than the almost 174,000 students participating in publicly funded private education programs, primarily with vouchers.[1]

Although he did not oppose school voucher programs,[2] Coulson sometimes rankled others in the school choice movement with his unvarnished criticism of their flaws. He readily conceded that there are tradeoffs—most notably regarding the simplicity of implementation and potential to scale up. But Coulson nevertheless argued forcefully that a system of tax credits for both parents and donors to scholarship organizations is superior to school vouchers for constitutional, philosophical, and policy reasons. In this chapter, I will revisit his central arguments for tax credits and concerns about public funding in light of the advent of a new educational choice mechanism: education savings accounts (ESAs).

In Search of Educational Excellence

In *Market Education*, Coulson analyzed education systems around the world and throughout history, from classical Greece to the present day, to determine what worked, what didn't, and why. After years of painstaking research, he concluded that the best education systems—regardless of culture or era—had five key elements: "choice and financial responsibility for parents, and freedom, competition, and the profit motive for schools—in essence, a free market in education."[3]

Coulson subsequently tested his theory by reviewing the global research. After analyzing more than 150 statistical comparisons across eight different educational outcomes, Coulson found that private schools consistently outperformed government-run schools, and that the most market-like education systems—those that had the five key elements he had previously identified—were even more likely to have a statistically significant advantage over state monopolies.[4]

Coulson's conclusions ran counter to the prevailing view of education, which had its roots in the ideas of Horace Mann and the "common school" reformers who built the system in which most American children are still educated. Their key premise, according to Coulson, was that "state-appointed experts would make better educational decisions for children than would those children's own parents."[5] Rather than having parents choose and pay for their children's schooling, Coulson wrote that Mann believed children should be sent to "a system of schools operated by the state, free of charge, with state-appointed experts overseeing their content, teacher training, and administration."[6] Since all the schools were held to the same standards and were publicly funded, there would be no need to compete, let alone earn profits.

By the modern era, Mann's views had become the conventional wisdom among the public schooling establishment. Coulson's read of the historical and international empirical evidence led him not only to reject Mann's views but also to criticize the approach of other ostensibly pro-market education reformers:

> Nearly all pundits and reformers assume that education markets compose a smorgasbord from which we can select or reject policy details according to personal taste or political expediency. This assumption, rarely acknowledged and never defended, is wrong. Properly functioning education markets much more closely resemble delicate ecosystems in which the alteration or removal of key elements leads to the decline or collapse of the entire system.[7]

For example, charter schools—long the darling of education reformers—are an improvement over the status quo, but they do not have all five elements that Coulson identified as necessary for a well-functioning market in education. Chartering may have expanded parents' options, exposed schools to greater competition, and even opened some opportunity for profit, but parents lack any financial responsibility and the level of school autonomy is far more limited than that enjoyed by private schools.

Although he believed they were superior to charters, Coulson also had concerns about private school vouchers. Historical experience in America and other countries suggested that government funding brought government control that often undermined the essential market mechanisms he had identified. Moreover, whereas the U.S. Supreme Court had ruled vouchers constitutional under the First Amendment, Coulson warned that provisions in state constitutions—particularly Blaine amendments and compelled support clauses—would prevent policymakers from enacting voucher programs, or at least limit them to a relatively small number of secular private schools. For that matter, Coulson was not entirely unsympathetic to the spirit of those constitutional provisions. He believed Thomas Jefferson was right in declaring that "to compel a man to furnish contributions of money for the propagation of opinions which he disbelieves and abhors, is sinful and tyrannical."[8]

By contrast, Coulson argued, tax credits avoid these issues because they involve having parents or donors spend their own money for educational purposes. No parent or taxpayer is compelled to contribute toward the propagation of ideas they dislike, which in turn means that the tax credits do not violate the Blaine Amendment or compelled support clauses. Moreover, policymakers are less likely to regulate parents' use of their own money (or that of a donor) than they are to regulate the use of public funds.

Although I had been a voucher proponent, Coulson's arguments persuaded me of the superiority of tax credits. I am similarly persuaded that publicly funded education savings accounts are superior to vouchers. Whereas vouchers are limited to schools, ESAs embody a more expansive vision of education that empowers parents to customize their child's education through tutoring, online courses, homeschool materials, and more. Likewise, because parents can use ESA funds to purchase a variety of educational goods and services and save unused funds for later, they do not create a voucher-style price floor and they encourage greater price-consciousness.

Someone who believes in the superiority of both tax credits and ESAs over traditional vouchers might logically conclude that the best vehicle for expanding educational choice would combine the two policies. As I have explained elsewhere, it is possible for policymakers to design ESA programs that are funded through tax credits for both parental contributions and third-party donations.[9] However, because public funding is more scalable and because some of the design features of ESAs may mitigate Coulson's primary concerns about constitutionality and the potential for over-regulation, it is worth reexamining the tradeoffs between tax credits and public funding.

Toward Market Education: Public Funding vs. Tax Credits

Coulson argued that funding private education through tax credits is superior to public funding because tax credits expand freedom of conscience for taxpayers, are more likely to be found constitutional, and are less likely to come with deleterious regulatory strings attached. In the following, I consider the merits of these arguments, especially as they pertain to ESAs.

Credits, Coercion, and Constitutionality

In its landmark decision *Zelman v. Simmons-Harris* (2002), the U.S. Supreme Court upheld the constitutionality of a school voucher program in Ohio against a First Amendment challenge. The Court ruled that the program was constitutional because it was "enacted for the valid secular purpose of providing educational assistance to poor children," that it was "neutral with respect to religion," and that any funds that indirectly reached a religious school were the incidental result of parents' "own genuine and independent private choice."[10]

Although vouchers do not implicate the Establishment Clause, all but three state constitutions contain a compelled support clause, a Blaine Amendment, or both. The former date back to the colonial era and generally forbid the state from compelling citizens to support religious institutions against their consent. The latter, named for the infamous nativist Sen. James G. Blaine of Maine, were primarily fueled by animus toward Catholics in the late 19th century and generally forbid the state from funding "sectarian" schools, a thinly veiled reference to Catholic schools in an era when the so-called common schools taught the Bible and prayed in accordance with nondenominational Protestant beliefs and practice.

Although those clauses can pose a significant hurdle to enacting publicly funded school choice programs—some state supreme courts have ruled that they prohibit vouchers—education tax credits have a perfect record of surviving such constitutional challenges because tax credits constitute private, not public, funds. However, Coulson was prone to overestimate the height of this hurdle. After the Supreme

Court of Wisconsin upheld the Milwaukee voucher program as constitutional under both its compelled support clause and Blaine Amendment in 1998, Coulson expressed surprise at their "inexplicable legal magic" and cautioned that "their dazzling léger-de-loi may be difficult to replicate."[11] However, replication was not as difficult as Coulson predicted. Since then, the high courts in Ohio (1999), Indiana (2013), Alabama (2015),[12] Oklahoma (2016), and Nevada (2016) have followed Wisconsin's lead in declaring publicly funded voucher programs constitutional. Only the state supreme court of Arizona and a plurality of the Colorado Supreme Court have cited these provisions to strike down voucher programs.

Upholding public funding under these constitutional provisions does not require "legal magic" but rather careful design. The Blaine amendments were intended to prohibit the direct funding of sectarian schools, but under school voucher programs, the state funds parents, not schools. The compelled support clauses were intended to prevent the state from establishing a religion, funding the church or ministries of religious groups, or compelling people to attend churches, as was often the practice in the early American colonies. School voucher programs, however, are religiously neutral—parents can choose to use the vouchers at schools representing a variety of religious affiliations or none at all. No one is compelled to attend a religious school against their consent, and the state neither favors nor disfavors any particular religion, or religion in general. Voters are no more compelled to support religious schooling via their taxes than they are compelled to support ideas they "disbelieve and abhor" taught in their local district school—a fact to which I will return in a moment. Depending on the phrasing of a particular state's constitutional provisions and its history of interpreting them, it is easy to see how school vouchers can be consistent with both the spirit and letter of most state constitutions. According to the Institute for Justice, the pro-liberty law firm with the most experience litigating school choice cases nationwide, beyond Colorado, there are only 17 states where these provisions likely prohibit public funding, which is fewer than half the states that have such constitutional provisions.[13] (In addition, Florida's supreme court struck down a voucher program under its uniformity clause in a deeply flawed decision that other states' high courts have not replicated.)

Moreover, publicly funded ESAs may survive constitutional challenges in places where vouchers would not. Although the Arizona

Supreme Court struck down a voucher program in 2009, it left an opening for ESAs. The court ruled in *Cain v. Horne* that the vouchers ran afoul of Arizona's Blaine Amendment because the funds could only be used for private-school tuition, and most of the private schools in the state were religiously affiliated. However, during oral arguments, even the petitioners agreed that if private-school tuition had been only one of many possible uses for the funds, the program would have passed constitutional muster. Choice advocates responded by proposing and eventually enacting an ESA plan that empowers parents to purchase a wide variety of educational products and services. After a lower court ruled Arizona's ESA constitutional in 2013, the state supreme court let the decision stand.

Whether other state supreme courts follow suit is yet to be seen, but there is reason to think that they might. All states have publicly funded programs that aid low-income citizens in obtaining basic goods and services, even from religiously affiliated providers or for religious purposes. Recipients of state-funded Medicaid vouchers can obtain services at Catholic hospitals with a priest on the staff and a crucifix in every room. They can use food vouchers for religious feasts. They can host religious services or Bible studies in their publicly subsidized homes. And even in states that don't have a state version of the Pell Grant, they can use welfare income to cover tuition at religious colleges or pre-K–12 schools.

Moreover, even if some state courts adopt a restrictive interpretation of their religion clauses, they may be overruled. The U.S. Supreme Court may soon consider two cases on the constitutionality of states' enacting aid programs that exclude groups because of their religious beliefs. In *Trinity Lutheran Church of Columbia v. Pauley*, the Court is asked to consider whether Missouri was constitutionally permitted to deny a church-affiliated daycare center's application to the state's Playground Scrap Tire Surface Material Grant Program solely because of its religious affiliation. Petitioners contend that the U.S. Constitution's Free Exercise and Establishment Clauses require the government to be neutral with regard to religion—as the Supreme Court has previously held in *Church of the Lukumi Babalu Aye, Inc. v. City of Hialeah* (1993) and other decisions—and therefore prohibit states from both favoring and disfavoring religious groups. As this book goes to print, the case has been granted certiorari, but oral arguments have not yet been scheduled. In *Douglas County School District v. Taxpayers for Public Education*, the Court is asked whether it was constitutional for a plurality of the Colorado Supreme Court to mandate the exclusion of religious schools from the Douglas County school voucher program under the state's Blaine Amendment. As in *Trinity*, the petitioners assert that the U.S. Constitution requires that such aid programs be religiously neutral. A judgment for the petitioners in either case (but particularly the second) would pave the way for publicly funded school choice programs to be constitutional in nearly every state.[14]

Constitutionality aside, Coulson still favored tax credits over public funding because the former do not compel taxpayers to financially support ideas they may find disagreeable. After the U.S. Supreme Court rejected a challenge to Arizona's scholarship tax credit program, he wrote the following:

> The Supreme Court's [*Arizona Christian School Tuition Organization v.*] *Winn* ruling reminds us . . . that there is a way to finance universal education without resorting to socially corrosive compulsion. Indeed if we wish our schools to promote mutual respect among people of different religions and world views, we must respect the right of parents to offer their children an education consistent with their values, and we must not compel taxpayers to support forms of instruction that violate their convictions. Tax credit programs such as Arizona's do both.[15]

Of course, as Coulson recognized, America's system of public schooling already compels taxpayers to support forms of instruction that violate their convictions. Coulson certainly preferred a system in which no one is compelled because financially supporting education is entirely voluntary, but that is not a politically viable option today or in the foreseeable future. The question before us is whether it is better (1) to compel all people (through their taxes) to support the one type of schooling that reflects the views of the majority (or a politically powerful minority), allowing them to support other educational views only through voluntary contributions; or (2) to allow all parents access to public funds to purchase instruction in line with their own convictions.

There is no obviously correct answer here. Enacting education tax credits alongside the existing government-run school system would, relative to vouchers, at least limit the types of instruction that taxpayers are compelled to support. But it is unequal in compelling everyone to support one type of education (the public school system) to the exclusion of all others. In a system of publicly funded choice, everyone is equally compelled to support all types of education, at least indirectly. Imagine a world in which nearly everyone agrees that the state must purchase a fruit for every citizen every day, and in which most people prefer apples but others prefer oranges, plums, or pears. Imagine further that the choice of one fruit offends the moral sensibilities of those who have different tastes. Would it be more just and fair to compel everyone to support the provision of apples while those who prefer other fruits must solicit their neighbors for tax credit–eligible donations? Or should an equal amount of public funds be allocated to each citizen to purchase the fruit of their choice? If ending all such compulsion (whether to support the purchase of fruit or education) is not politically viable, it is understandable why even the most ardent libertarians might prefer the second option.

Coulson was right that tax credits could survive constitutional scrutiny even in states where vouchers could not, although his assessment of the constitutional threat to public funding was overstated. In states that are constitutionally forbidden from publicly funding school choice programs, tax credits are obviously the superior (and perhaps only) alternative.[16] Nevertheless, public funding is constitutional in about four-fifths of states, and the U.S. Supreme Court may strike down state constitutional provisions that mandate active discrimination against religious groups in otherwise neutral aid programs. Coulson was also right that tax credits entail less coercion, in that no one is compelled to support private education through their taxes. But so long as everyone is compelled to support some types of education through their taxes, it is not clear that granting public funding to some but not others is more just or fair. In states where public funding is constitutional, policymakers should primarily consider the policy implications of choosing public funding or tax credits.

The Elements of a Market in Education

In his essay, "On the Way to School," Coulson asked, "Is there any sort of financial assistance program that can ensure universal access to a free education marketplace without destroying the conditions necessary for that market to survive and thrive?"[17] As noted, Coulson identified five key elements necessary for a well-functioning market in education: parental choice and financial responsibility, instructional freedom for schools, competition, and the profit motive. Additionally, the market must be large enough to ensure robust competition among a wide and diverse set of educational options. Small choice programs do little more than fill empty seats at existing private schools. Universal access is required to unleash the dynamism and innovation that make choice and competition meaningful. The ideal choice program, therefore, would provide sufficient funding for universal access to a quality education without undermining the key elements of an effective market in education. As Coulson wrote,

> What really matters, from a policy standpoint, is how many additional families a program helps to gain access to the education marketplace, and what its prospects are for growth in that area. This is a function of several factors, including the average benefit size, average private school tuition, the number of participating families and the prospects for growth in that number. The program that will allow the most people to gain access to the education marketplace is not necessarily the one that has the biggest total dollar value (average benefit size multiplied by program enrollment), but the one that lowers the perceived cost of private schooling in a meaningful way for the most families.[18]

Even setting aside programs for students with special needs, the value of the average voucher is more than double the value of the average tax credit scholarship nationwide (about $6,300 versus about $2,500 in the 2015–16 academic year).[19] And although more students in the United States are receiving tax credit scholarships than vouchers, there's some evidence that voucher programs scale up faster. Indiana's tax credit scholarship program launched in 2010, and enrollment peaked at just over 11,000 in 2013–14 before declining to just under 9,500 in 2014–15.[20] Indiana's voucher program launched in 2011, and enrollment surpassed 30,000 students in the same time period.[21] Likewise, Louisiana's tax credit scholarship program took effect in 2012 and served fewer than 800 students in 2015–16, whereas more than 7,000 students participate in the state's voucher program.[22] Of course, it's possible—even likely—that the voucher programs are "cannibalizing" participation in the tax credit scholarship programs because they are worth more money (about 40 percent more in Louisiana and nearly 2.5 times as much in Indiana), but the higher values also likely attract more participants in total.

Although not conclusive, the evidence suggests that publicly funded programs are more likely to provide more money to more students than tax credits (although still significantly less per pupil than what the district schools spend, meaning that higher participation will produce a net savings to taxpayers) and to scale up more quickly. The question then becomes whether the increased participation from public funding is undermined by the regulatory strings that might come attached.

In theory, it is possible for states to regulate schools even without providing them any financial support, either through vouchers or tax credits, and in some states the regulatory burden is substantial even in the absence of school choice programs. However, it is also true that school choice programs tend to include some amount of additional regulations. In 2011, Coulson conducted a statistical analysis of existing voucher and scholarship tax credit programs to determine which ones were more likely to include regulations that undermine the elements of a well-functioning market in education. These regulations included price controls, admissions requirements, curriculum regulations, testing mandates, barriers to entry, restrictions on religious freedom, staffing regulations, financial regulations, and facilities regulations. The study found that "vouchers, but not tax credits, impose a substantial and statistically significant additional regulatory burden on participating private schools," especially in terms of price controls (requiring that schools not charge more than the value of the voucher), admissions (requiring voucher-accepting schools to have an open admissions policy), and testing mandates.[23] Although the sample size was relatively small, Coulson noted that the "variation in regulation within states is much greater than the variation between states," indicating that policymakers tend to approach the two types of choice policies differently.

In 2014, the Friedman Foundation for Educational Choice (now EdChoice) published a study by Andrew D. Catt that largely reached the same conclusion as Coulson. Notably, Catt found that most of the regulations that private schools face were in place before the enactment of any school choice program, although vouchers did tend to increase the regulatory burden. Tax credits, by contrast, were given a lighter regulatory touch. In Catt's scoring system, voucher programs had "regulatory impact scores slightly more than three times as negative as the scores of tax-credit scholarship programs."[24] When controlling for outliers, such as programs for students with special needs, the voucher scores were five times as negative as the tax credits. Catt's study was also the first to look at the regulatory impact of the first education savings account program in Arizona and concluded that it was the least regulated of any choice program in the country.

Of course, it is impossible to generalize from a single program. However, since then, four more states have adopted ESAs: Florida, Mississippi, Nevada, and Tennessee. As in Arizona, none have price controls or admissions requirements, although Florida, Nevada, and Tennessee require that students take their choice of the state test or a nationally norm-referenced test. However, the state does not impose any consequences on the students or on any private schools or other education providers related to the test results.

This is no mere coincidence. The regulatory framework of the existing ESA programs reflects both their underlying theory and practical difficulties in attaching voucher-style regulations to ESAs. ESAs are supposed to be an evolution from "school choice" to "educational choice," recognizing that not all formal education must take place in a traditional school classroom. ESAs empower parents to choose among a wide variety of educational products and services, including tutors, textbooks, online courses, homeschool curricula, educational therapy, and more—either in addition to or instead of private school tuition. The regulatory framework that has developed to regulate schools is not easily transferred to these other education providers.

Take testing, for example. For both vouchers and tax credit scholarships, it is relatively easy for policymakers to mandate that schools administer the state test, and then reward or punish them on the basis of the results. By contrast, with ESAs, that is practically impossible. When a student spends part of her day in a traditional school, part of the day taking courses online, part of the day with a tutor, and part of the day studying a homeschool curriculum, which of those education providers is the state supposed to hold responsible for that student's test scores? Policymakers can still mandate that students take a standardized test; but if they can't hold any particular provider primarily accountable for the results, the mandate is unlikely to create the sort of perverse incentives to narrow the curriculum and teach to the test that we have seen arise elsewhere. Instead, the tests merely provide parents with information that they likely desired anyway, which they can then factor in among the many other variables that are important to them.

Similarly, it is more difficult for policymakers to impose price controls on ESAs. As it is, ESAs are superior to traditional vouchers because they do not create a price floor. They're also less likely to create price ceilings. Although it is technically possible for policymakers to cap private school tuition at the full amount of the annual ESA allocations, doing so would not make much sense. The purpose of an ESA is to empower parents to customize their child's education using a wide variety of products and services. It is beyond the ability of policymakers to control the prices for all of these. Setting the maximum price for tuition is politically and practically feasible, if unwise. Setting a maximum price for all tutors, textbooks, online courses, educational therapies, and so on is neither politically nor practically feasible. Because policymakers are unlikely to attempt to control the price of only one of numerous categories of eligible purchases, ESAs do not pose the same threat as vouchers.

The same goes for admissions requirements. It is relatively easy for policymakers to require that all schools accepting vouchers (or even tax credit scholarships) admit all students who apply or hold a lottery if there is oversubscription. However, it is politically and practically difficult to do so for every tutor or online course, and no state has even attempted it.

The technocratic reformers who support additional choice along with additional state regulations recognize the difficulty with imposing their preferred regulatory framework on ESAs, which is why their support for ESA initiatives has been tepid at best. In Nevada, some technocratic school choice advocates refused to support or even openly opposed the ESA legislation.[25] Of course, what they see as a bug is really a feature.

Conclusion: Forging a New Consensus

It remains to be seen whether publicly funded ESAs will be able to provide universal access to a free market in education without introducing harmful regulations that undermine that market. As outlined in this chapter, there are reasons for optimism. But anyone who has studied Coulson's work knows there are also reasons for skepticism. Of course, even in the absence of educational choice policies, there are no guarantees that the state will refrain from imposing well-intentioned but misguided regulations—the price of educational freedom is eternal vigilance.

Like Coulson, we should rigorously examine the evidence before us in pursuit of the ideal education system—one that provides every child with access to a high-quality education that meets his or her unique learning needs. Coulson's pioneering work examining education systems across the globe and throughout history has shown that such a system would give parents both choice and responsibility and give education providers freedom to determine their own curricula and earn a profit in a competitive environment. Education reformers today may or may not reach the same conclusions as Coulson as to which policies best embody the elements he identified, but we are all forever indebted to him for his contributions to the pursuit of educational excellence.

5. On Coulson's Historical Perspective

Jay P. Greene and Jason Bedrick

Current education policy debates seem to have little use for historical analysis. We leap into a brave new world with little concern for what has happened before. And as long as our program evaluations show positive results (and sometimes even that doesn't matter), we feel confident that we are guided by science even if we ignore the past. Andrew Coulson's scholarship serves as a reminder to the education policy world how important studying history remains despite advances in rigorous empirical analysis. This is true for several reasons, which we will enumerate in this chapter.

History as a Guide for the Future

First, program evaluations do not tell us what programs should be implemented so that they can be studied. Before we assess the effectiveness of any intervention, we first have to decide that an intervention is worth trying. There were no evaluations of private school choice before policymakers adopted the Milwaukee voucher program. There were no studies on the effects of charter schools before Minnesota first tried them.

While those exact programs had never been tried before, they were not completely lacking in historical antecedents. As Coulson described in his book, *Market Education: The Unknown History*, private markets for education existed and thrived in the past in a variety of cultures and eras from ancient Greece to modern Japan. Although no single case study can conclusively demonstrate the effectiveness of a particular system or intervention, patterns of results spanning time and cultures are suggestive. As Coulson explained,

> If a particular approach to organizing and funding schools consistently works well across widely varying circumstances, and if it consistently outperforms other systems when operating in similar circumstances, we can be confident that this pattern of results is due to the system itself, and not simply an accident of circumstance. In fact, the greater the cultural and economic

> differences among the nations and historical periods studied, the more compelling any consistent pattern of results becomes.[1]

The divergent education systems in cosmopolitan Athens and militant Sparta make for a useful comparison. The Spartan government exercised complete control over every boy's education, training each for battle in state-run boarding facilities starting at age seven. Athenians took a more laissez-faire approach. Teachers like Socrates were free to start their own schools and set their own curricula. Their success depended on their ability to attract students, which meant that they had to not only keep their fees competitive, but also teach the content and skills that parents desired for their children. Whereas the mostly illiterate Spartans languished in a cultural and economic backwater, the highly literate Athenians produced a thriving economy and made great contributions to philosophy, science, and the arts that are still admired today.

America has its own history of market education. At the time of the American Revolution, education in many towns was "financed by a combination of tuition charges and local taxes, which allowed some of the poorer students to attend for free while those who could afford to largely paid their own way."[2] Although not exactly vouchers or charter schools, these examples can provide at least some support to largely theoretical arguments for experimenting with new school choice arrangements. Historical analyses cannot prove the effectiveness of any particular policy, but they can at least suggest what policies are possible and might be desirable.

Thinking Outside Existing Arrangements

Second, historical analyses help reveal what aspects of current arrangements may or may not be necessary for achieving certain policy goals. We grow accustomed so quickly to education policies that we often forget that they did not always exist. The existence of state educational standards goes back only a few decades, but some who debate current education policy seem to have difficulty imagining how schools could operate without being told what to teach by state or even national officials. Nationwide, schools have been state-operated for barely more than a century, yet many people have trouble conceiving how the state might change its role from operating schools to just helping pay for them. We are falsely told that state-operated schools are the foundation of our democracy, ignoring that Horace Mann didn't start the push for public schools until more than half a century after the Republic's founding.

Not only were Americans able to articulate democratic ideals, engage in a revolution to achieve them, and operate a fairly successful Republic without any state-operated schools, but also levels of literacy were generally quite high in the absence of state schooling. By the time the U.S. Constitution was drafted in 1787, about two-thirds of free men were literate nationwide, and that ratio was closer to 80 percent in New England. By 1850, before "common schools" were widespread, only about 1 in 10 people identified themselves as illiterate on the U.S. census.[3]

A similar pattern was evident across the pond. As Coulson noted in his analysis of English education, "Clearly the spread of literacy up to the 1830s was achieved in spite of, rather than thanks to, state intervention."[4] The English did not begin publicly subsidizing education until 1833, and state-run schools were not introduced until 1870. By that time, English men were nearly universally literate, and "virtually all children were receiving some schooling."[5] Although the goal of Forster's Education Act of 1870 was, ostensibly, to expand access to education among the poor, the newly created system of state-subsidized schools mainly just cannibalized private school enrollment. By then, even the poorest and least-educated parents in Britain commonly enrolled their children at fee-charging private schools. About a decade after the introduction of state-run schools, the rate of children receiving an education was about the same, but the private schools had mostly closed down. "In essence," Coulson observed, "government intervention in education served primarily to extinguish private schools, rather than to increase the percentage of children receiving an education."[6]

History is not a steady march of progress with all government programs improving our lives. Sometimes those programs have made our lives worse or played no role in the progress that was otherwise occurring. By studying history we not only learn what policies might be possible and desirable, but we also gain insight into what policies might not be necessary or inevitable. If we once were able to live well without a government program, perhaps we could again live very well without it. Empirical evaluations, unlike historical analyses, cannot tell us what policies to try or what policies we might be able to do without.

By the same token, historical analyses can help us identify conditions that are necessary for a well-functioning education system. At the conclusion of his book, Coulson argued that at least five key elements have proven necessary across centuries and continents for an effective market in education: parental choice, parental financial responsibility, educational freedom, competition, and the profit motive. When parents can choose their child's learning environment, they tend to be more involved with their child's education, and the schools are more likely to keep pace with the needs of the times—so long as they have the freedom to do so. The more options there are, the greater the pressure to meet parents' needs at a reasonable price. However, he who pays the school piper calls the instructional tune; the price of parental control is bearing at least some financial responsibility. And finally, allowing schools to seek profits fosters innovation, encourages greater efficiency and cost control, and provides an incentive to scale up.

When one or more of these elements are not present, the effectiveness of the market is diminished. Louisiana's voucher program, for example, contains a host of regulations that diminish or eliminate these features. By requiring voucher-accepting schools to administer the state test, the state indirectly restricts the schools' freedom to set their own curriculum. In capping the price of tuition and forbidding schools from charging parents more than the value of the voucher, the program effectively eliminates any parental financial responsibility. By mandating open admissions, the state essentially prevents schools from determining their own character or identity, thereby narrowing the diversity of options available to parents. As a consequence of these regulations, only about one-third of private schools in Louisiana have been willing to accept the vouchers. No one who has read *Market Education* will be surprised to learn that the first—and so far only—negative results obtained from a random-assignment study of a voucher program were in Louisiana.[7]

Figuring Out What's Important

Third, we need historical analyses to help us decide which outcomes we should even be examining in our program evaluations. Rigorous evaluations provide a method for identifying the effects of policies, but they don't tell us which effects are important. These days, we typically focus on evaluating how policy interventions affect test scores, but we do so largely because test results are readily available, not because they are strongly predictive of later life outcomes or capturing things that matter most. As we learn from Coulson's historical work, the important effects of government education policies often involve suppressing political dissent, favoring particular religious views, and controlling economic activity. These effects matter enormously to people and yet are virtually never captured in program evaluations.

To this day, public schools are widely assumed to be a unifying force in our diverse society, the supposed "cornerstone of democracy," where students of all colors and creeds come together. In fact, as Coulson meticulously details, public schooling has often been the source of social strife. Before the rise of public schooling, parents enrolled their children in schools that aligned with their values and matched their educational preferences. Far from producing the "balkanization" feared today, history shows us that diverse communities could live together in harmony when they did not have to struggle with their neighbors over what their children were taught:

> In areas where schools of different sects coexisted, they and their patrons seldom came into conflict, since they did not try to foist their views on one another. They lived and let live in what were comparatively stable, though increasingly diverse, communities. It was only after the state began creating uniform institutions for all children that these families were thrown into conflict.[8]

By its very nature, state control over schooling produces winners and losers in a diverse society. Public schools pit parents with conflicting views about education against each other in a struggle to have their views and values taught to their children—and everyone else's:

> Within public schools, many parents were faced with an unpleasant choice: accept that objectionable ideas would be forced on their children, or force their own ideas on everyone else's children by taking control of the system. It was this artificial choice between two evils that led to the Philadelphia Bible Riots, the beatings of Catholic children, the official denigration of immigrant values and lifestyles in public schools and textbooks, and laws—which would today be viewed as utterly unconstitutional—forcing the Protestant Bible on all families. The unpardonable treatment of black families by government schools, which persisted for over a century, does nothing to lighten this grim picture.[9]

We don't have Bible riots anymore—thank heaven—but parents still find plenty to fight about, whether it be pedagogy, sex ed, the science curriculum, freedom of expression, what constitutes appropriate reading material, and so on. If social harmony is one of our goals, the study of history is a better guide than any regression analysis.

Learning from Past Mistakes

Fourth, a study of history can help us avoid the mistakes of the past. Wave after wave of education reformers have promised utopia only to have their hopes and dreams dashed against the rocky shoals of reality. All too often, the reformers' failure has stemmed, in part, from the hubristic assumption that they knew better than parents. The declaration by the California State Superintendent of Public Instruction in 1864 that children "should be taught to consider [their] instructor, in many respects, superior to the parent in point of authority," or the Wisconsin Teachers' Association's assertion that "children are the property of the state" are notions that have currency even today.[10] Rather than attempt to persuade parents to embrace their vision, reformers have instead attempted to force them to comply. As Coulson details—in a book, it should be remembered, published before the era of Common Core or No Child Left Behind—reformers' attempts to circumvent parents tend to fail.

Education reformers talk a lot about the future of education but not enough about the past. As we seek to improve or redesign the system we have, we would do well to study how and why we got here, and how education systems developed differently elsewhere. Historical analysis can provide a deeper understanding of what features of our education system are necessary or superfluous and give us a broader perspective as to the outcomes we should seek to evaluate. A better understanding of history would also instill a vital sense of humility about what reformers can accomplish, especially through the clumsy hand of the state. In *Market Education* and his subsequent work, Andrew Coulson contributed mightily toward developing that understanding. May his legacy inspire us to continue down the path he illuminated.

6. Education, Markets, and Governments: Andrew Coulson's Global Research Agenda and Legacy

James Tooley

The last time I spent with Andrew Coulson was in 2014, at a small dinner in Hyderabad, India. We were celebrating the completion of his filming of low-cost private schools in poor parts of Hyderabad's Old City. These were some of the schools I had written about extensively in *The Beautiful Tree*.[1] Coulson had described me in an article about my work as "a 21st-century Indiana Jones," who travels to "the remotest regions on Earth researching something many regard as mythical." That mythical something was low-cost schools, which many refused to believe in even after I'd been presenting evidence on them for some years.[2]

I liked that image of myself, that identity Coulson had given me. Indiana Jones said, "If you want to be a good archaeologist, you gotta get out of the library," and Coulson believed this to be true for education policy as well. For his film on school choice—his magnum opus, *School Inc.: Taking Educational Excellence from Candle to Flame*—he was most definitely out of the ivory tower, engaging with those involved in educational entrepreneurship all over the world, including some of its poorest places. He had an abiding interest in markets in education wherever they could be found, learning lessons for their own sake and also for influencing the American school choice debate.

In this chapter, I will point to some of Coulson's enduring research in this area of international education, to give a flavor of some of his concerns, to inspire us to go back to his original work, and to explore further research questions that grow out of his legacy. I will explore two of his major themes: first, the dangers of government control of curriculum and, second, comparisons between government and market systems of education. I'll conclude by summarizing some findings about markets in education in some of the poorest parts of the world, which considerably interested Andrew Coulson.

Dangers of Government Control of Curriculum

A major theme in Coulson's work was the danger inherent in government control of curriculum. It is a theme in his magisterial *Market Education: The Unknown History*,[3] in which he traced the history of governments across time and place controlling curriculum for purposes of indoctrination. He brought that same theme up to date in his Cato Policy Analysis, "Education and Indoctrination in the Muslim World," and it continues to grow in relevance. He wrote in the latter:

> State-run schooling has always been one of the primary tools of tyrants. One of the most common first steps of would-be dictators is to shut down or take over private schools and then infuse the system with a curriculum that consolidates support for their regimes and agendas. Lycurgus did it in the Greek city-state of Sparta two and one-half millennia ago, Stalin, Hitler, Mao, Castro and Saddam Hussein all did it in the 20th century.[4]

Harvard University's Lant Pritchett has pointed to similar evidence of state-run schooling, including in Japan during the early Meiji period and Turkey under Atatürk, where the government imperative seems to be to control the curriculum for purposes of socialization and indoctrination. He suggests that the desire for such control is an inevitability of government education. Pritchett's argument is complex but is based on the premise that "instruction in beliefs is not third-party contractible, so organizations will choose to make, not buy, the inculcation of beliefs."[5] Essentially, given that governments of nation-states want appropriately socialized populations, and given the emergence of schooling as a useful vehicle for that socialization, governments will inevitably use public schooling for the purpose of socialization. In its extreme manifestations, that will mean schooling for the purposes of indoctrination. There is nothing much we can do about this inevitability.

Although Coulson did not comment specifically on Pritchett's work, his own writing makes clear that he would have thought Pritchett guilty of a naturalistic fallacy here: moving from "is" to "ought." Yes, Coulson certainly agreed that this is what governments have done, historically and globally, and are still doing. They control the curriculum of education and use it for socialization and, at worst, indoctrination. But Coulson's purpose in highlighting and exposing this tendency appears to have been precisely because he believed that with vigilance we can help challenge and combat it for the sake of educational freedom.

In particular, his comments about private education in this context suggest that he saw private education as a viable route away from government control, including control of the curriculum and its potential connection with indoctrination.

Coulson gave some chilling examples of recent ways in which the United States has been involved not only in this socialization process for itself, but also in using education for indoctrination in other countries. This happened in the late 20th century through America's "manipulation of Pakistan's Islamist madrasas."[6] As a result of the Soviet Union's invasion of Afghanistan, President Jimmy Carter sought to cause covert damage to Soviet operations, in part through a process of indoctrination in Pakistani schools. "Between 1986 and 1992, USAID [the United States Agency for International Development] underwrote the printing of explicitly violent Islamic textbooks for elementary school children," Coulson wrote.[7] The "recurrent theme" of these textbooks aimed at children in the first through sixth grades, "was the promotion of Islam through violence."[8] He noted that these textbooks took "rather a different tack than Dr. Seuss," assigning letters of the alphabet to words for Allah and jihad and so on.[9] Even in subjects that one might have thought relatively immune to this treatment, indoctrination seems to have been rampant. Here is an example from a fourth-grade mathematics text:

> The speed of a Kalashnikov bullet is 800 meters per second. . . . If a Russian is at a distance of 3,200 meters from a mujahid, and that mujahid aims at the Russian's head, calculate how many seconds it will take for the bullet to strike the Russian in the forehead.[10]

Clearly, Coulson remarked, this kind of U.S. intervention was morally wrong: "Whereas adult mujaheddin could freely choose whether or not to fight the Soviets, we helped them rob their children of that free will, molding them into jihadis before they were old enough to think for themselves. This put us in the company of the most wicked dictators in history."[11] Funding indoctrinating textbooks was also misguided pragmatically: "Whatever short-term benefit they may have provided in helping to halt Soviet expansionism is clearly outweighed by the generations of violent Islamists these books have helped to create."[12] The textbooks apparently remain "popular with militant Islamists in northern Pakistan," although now they are reprinted unofficially and "no longer at U.S. expense."[13]

Changing times brought changing needs. In 2003, under President George W. Bush, USAID changed tack and committed to fund the Pakistani government's Education Sector Reform strategy. This time the emphasis was on countering militant Islam by improving government schools, rather than on promoting it as before. Coulson thought this approach was misguided too, innocent of the way that Pakistan government–controlled curriculum took socialization to high levels: "Even Pakistan's most recent post-ESR [Education Sector Reform] textbooks instill animosity toward and mistrust of Hindus and Indians, glorify jihad and martyrdom in the name of Allah, encourage militarism, contain devotional religious instruction, and are insensitive to Pakistan's religious diversity."[14]

Coulson believed this tack—and a similar one in Iraq, where the American government was trying to impose a centralized schooling system, open to the danger of mass indoctrination—was entirely wrong. It focused on what governments demand from education rather than on what parents seek for their children. The alternative, he said, is to look to the private sector. Private schools across the developing world, he said, "are consistently more responsive to parents' demands. As a result, these schools are far less likely to try to indoctrinate children. . . . When choosing and paying for their own children's education, parents in these countries overwhelmingly seek out practical academic instruction and career training that will allow their children to become economically successful."[15]

I believe this area requires further reflection. In practice, whatever demands parents make for their children's curriculum, private schools often seem to be heavily constrained by government curricula, particularly in the developing world. Following government curriculum and associated assessments is usually a condition of official school recognition, and recognition is required for a school's students to take exams and so on.[16] Further research and development are needed to explore Coulson's ideas in this area. For example, to what extent are private schools currently subject to government curriculum with its potential for indoctrination? And to what extent can private schools break free from this curriculum, experimenting with their own ways of meeting parental demand? These important questions, which Coulson's work has illuminated, require careful deliberation.

Comparisons between Government and Market Systems of Education

When pointing to private education in his work on curriculum and indoctrination, Coulson was very clear on private schooling's virtues: "The biggest lesson of the research comparing alternative school governance structures is that fee-charging market schools out-perform government schools . . . in academic achievement, cost-effectiveness, facilities condition and maintenance, gender equity, and enrollment growth."[17] He presented the evidence for this most simply and lucidly in his article "Comparing Public, Private, and Market Schools: The International Evidence,"[18] which takes further the arguments raised in his contribution to the Cato volume *What America Can Learn from School Choice in Other Countries*.[19]

The key insight of his article is his realization that evidence from government-imposed school choice programs in America and elsewhere cannot inform our understanding of what real market education can offer. No American school choice program has created "a truly free and competitive education marketplace," typically because too many regulations have been imposed on both the supply and the demand sides.[20] School systems, even those featuring some aspects of school choice reforms, Coulson realized, "differ from free and competitive markets in crucial ways," including lack of "profit, price change, market entry, and product differentiation."[21] There are, in fact, education systems that approximate real markets much more closely elsewhere in the world, and Coulson turned to them in his review of the evidence.

One approach is to look at how different nations—with different mixes of public and private schools—perform on specific international tests, such as the Program for International Student Assessment or the Trends in International Mathematics and Science Study. But Coulson rightly eschewed that approach, as "nations differ substantially in factors related to educational outcomes (e.g., wealth, culture, demographics)" and it makes little sense to assume that student performance on these international tests "is due to that nation's school system alone."[22] To overcome "the hurdle posed by cultural and economic differences between countries," Coulson proposed comparing "different sorts of school systems *within nations*"[23] (emphasis added). A study comparing private and public education within a country such as India, for instance, would avoid the problem of bringing in international differences in wealth, culture, demography, and so on.

Of course, such a study will only point to the relative performance of public and private school systems within that nation and so will not immediately be generalizable. However, Coulson argued that if similar results are repeated across nations, then "we can be fairly confident that the observed pattern is the result of the system itself" and not simply geographical circumstance.[24] With these considerations in mind, Coulson conducted a systematic literature review of all available evidence comparing public and private schooling. His initial analysis covered 65 studies from more than 20 countries, with 156 separate findings in the areas of academic achievement (as measured by student test scores), efficiency (measured as academic achievement per dollar spent per pupil), and parental satisfaction, as well five other factors that appear less frequently in the literature.[25] Using a simple "vote counting" procedure, Coulson showed that these studies demonstrate overwhelmingly the advantages of the private sector in education: 106 studies showed significant private-school advantage, 37 were statistically insignificant, and 13 showed significant government-school advantage overall.

Coulson was not entirely satisfied with this result, however, as he recognized that some of the studies may have featured private schools operating under conditions of subsidy and/or heavy regulation, not in genuine market systems. Eliminating those cases, he was left with 76 studies, which showed an even more striking private-market advantage: 59 studies were statistically significant in favor of markets, 13 were statistically insignificant, and only 4 showed a significant government advantage, using the same set of comparison characteristics previously noted. Coulson summarized the findings thus:

> In more than 150 statistical comparisons covering eight different educational outcomes, the private sector outperforms the public sector in the overwhelming majority of cases. Moreover, this margin of superiority is greatest when the freest and most market-like private schools are compared to the least open and least competitive government systems.[26]

One possibility that might make these findings misleading, Coulson conceded, came from the potential for "selection bias," which "occurs when families choose public or private schools because of personal characteristics related to educational outcomes, and researchers fail to control for those characteristics."[27] If more-motivated parents "disproportionately choose private schools, then the private sector will enjoy an academic advantage that must be controlled for in order to make a fair comparison between the sectors."[28]

However, several of the studies did take selection bias into account. Coulson pointed to examples from India, Indonesia, Colombia, the Dominican Republic, the Philippines, Thailand, Tanzania, and Nigeria. Interestingly, the impact of controlling for selection bias is not straightforwardly against private education, as might be anticipated. In countries such as Tanzania and Indonesia, for instance, where access to public secondary schooling is based on pupil achievement in primary school, "controlling for selection bias tends to favor the private sector."[29]

Moreover, selection bias may not be as large a problem as many commentators believe. Because the studies are of places where the vast majority of children go to private schools, the private schools dominate the field. Coulson argued that commentators find it difficult to shake off the notion "that private school families are fundamentally different from public school families." They assume that those using private schools are "a small, elite pool of committed parents and that it is their commitment and not a private sector effect" that leads to the striking private school advantage.[30]

If that commitment effect were correct, Coulson wrote, then "we would expect the education market's advantage over monopoly schooling to decline as private sector enrollment share rises, and eventually to be eliminated or even reversed in cases where private sector enrollment share exceeded public sector enrollment share."[31] If the private market in education were serving most families, then "the impact of a small elite of committed parents on its overall performance would be greatly attenuated and perhaps erased."[32]

The evidence seems to support this suggestion. Coulson pointed to studies from urban Lucknow, India, for instance, where approximately 80 percent of the students were enrolled in private (aided and unaided) schools, yet the private schools outperformed the government schools. Similar results were found in Nigeria and in other Indian cities.

Here is an important and original idea that challenges the assumption that selectivity bias skews the results of public-private comparisons: When private schools are patronized by a "small, especially committed elite," then one would expect selectivity bias to enter the picture. However, when the vast majority of children are enrolled in private schools, and the private schools still outperform government schools, then "it is no longer reasonable to ascribe the market's advantage to some special indefinable quality of a parental elite."[33]

It is these kinds of educational markets—where a vast majority of children, including the poor, attend private school—that Coulson pointed to in his conclusion. He recommended *The Beautiful Tree* for those readers "interested in learning more about these entrepreneurial schools serving the third world poor."[34]

As this was clearly an area that greatly interested and excited Andrew Coulson (it was the reason, for instance, that he finished filming his school choice documentary in the slums of Hyderabad), let me conclude by summarizing some of the findings of my book and how the research has developed since it was published.

The Revolution of Low-Cost Private Schools

I directed two major research programs, funded by the John Templeton Foundation, on low-cost private schools. The first took place between 2003 and 2005 and the second between 2011 and 2013. This research showed private schools burgeoning in poor communities across sub-Saharan Africa and South Asia rather than existing only to serve elites—the point that Andrew Coulson noted. The first research program explored India (Delhi and Hyderabad), Kenya (Nairobi), Ghana (Ga, near Accra), and Nigeria (Lagos State), as well as rural India (Mahbubnagar) and China (Gansu Province). The research found that the majority of schoolchildren (up to 75 percent) in urban and peri-urban communities attended low-cost private schools, while a significant minority (about 30 percent) in rural communities attended private schools.

The sheer number of low-cost private schools is staggering. In India alone, I estimated there were approximately 300,000 at the time of the research, and the number has likely grown. One state in Nigeria, Lagos, has an estimated 14,000 low-cost private schools. We tested about 24,000 children in mathematics, English, and one other subject and typically found that children in low-cost private schools outperformed those in government schools, even after controlling for family-background variables and possible selectivity biases.[35]

The second study extended the focus of research to conflict and post-conflict countries in sub-Saharan Africa. In Liberia, we conducted a school survey in seven major slums in Monrovia, followed by a household survey in one of those slums.[36] The survey found 432 schools serving a total of 102,205 pupils in the seven slums. Of these schools, only two were government-run. Schools run as for-profit ventures made up 57.2 percent of all schools found, with 60.7 percent of all pupils. The rest were run by various nonprofit secular and religious groups. The household survey showed that, for children aged 5 to 14, 8.2 percent were in government schools, 71.0 percent were in private schools, and 20.9 percent were out of school.

In Sierra Leone, we set out to find all schools serving children of primary-school age in Western Area (both the Western Area Rural district and the Western Area Urban district).[37] We tested more than 3,000 "primary 4" (4th grade) students in English and mathematics in a random sample of schools, stratified by management categories, and we created multilevel models to analyze the data. Government was found to manage 10 percent of all schools, with 90 percent managed by the private sector. For-profit schools made up the largest proportion of schools (33 percent of all schools), followed by established churches (17 percent).

Regarding achievement, we found that an average child was predicted to perform better in private than in government schools. For English (reading), an average boy in a government school was predicted to achieve 15.5 percent of total answers correct, while a girl would achieve 10.8 percent. In a low-cost private school, the boy's result would nearly double; the girl's result would nearly triple, to 30.2 percent in a for-profit school or 29.0 percent in a nonprofit school.

In South Sudan, we carried out a survey to locate all schools in the urban and peri-urban areas of Juba.[38] We found 199 schools serving a total of 88,820 pupils at nursery, primary, and high school levels. The private sector accounted for 73.9 percent of the schools and 62.6 percent of the pupils. The largest category of schools by number was private proprietor schools (28.1 percent) followed by government (26.1 percent).

Low-cost private schools are affordable to the poor—not surprising given their ubiquity in poor areas. We defined affordability on the basis of what poor families could afford for all their children if they were to spend a maximum of 10 percent of their income on school fees and associated costs.[39] "Lowest-cost" and "low-cost" private schools are those affordable to families on, respectively, the internationally recognized $1.25 and $2 per person per day poverty lines (at 2005 exchange rates and purchasing power parity). In the slums of Monrovia, Liberia, for instance, the vast majority (73.7 percent) of private schools we found were "lowest cost"; in our Sierra Leone study, 66 percent of for-profit private schools were "lowest cost." Indeed, the cost to parents of sending a child to a government school averages (in the Monrovia, Liberia, study) about 75 percent of the cost of sending a child to a low-cost private school once all of the extra costs of schooling—uniforms, books, exam fees, transportation, and so on—are taken into account.

All of the research shows a considerable success story. Even in some of the poorest, most conflict-affected places on earth, educational entrepreneurs have created low-cost private schools, which are serving the majority of children in urban areas, and serving them better than the public schools. To me—as to Andrew Coulson—the existence and success of these low-cost private schools was something to be greatly celebrated.

However, this position is controversial. The literature reveals a hugely polarized debate about the significance of low-cost private schools. Why the controversy? A decade ago I used the phrase "de facto privatization" to describe the low-cost private school movement; the phrase is now in wide circulation.[40] But the term carries huge significance. Privatization, the assigning of businesses or services to private rather than state ownership, is normally considered a top-down approach (governments "denationalize" particular industries, such as railways or steel). "De facto" privatization, in contrast, occurs from the bottom up, as when the people themselves, not the state—indeed, often against the wishes of the state—engage in reassigning education to private rather than state control and ownership. Controversy seems to stem from the realization that the people themselves are embracing a solution to educational delivery that differs from the accepted wisdom that has been in place since 1948 (with the Universal Declaration of Human Rights). The accepted wisdom was that government should be the supplier of schools to the poor. A lot is at stake if the people themselves appear to be rejecting that consensus.

Coulson was no stranger to this controversy. He engaged in the public debates in a surefooted and engaging manner, using research-based evidence to fuel his arguments. The debates continue. For instance, I recently published an article about a paper that employed what is widely hailed as the gold standard for research in this area, a "randomized controlled trial" voucher experiment, in Andhra Pradesh, India.[41] The findings showed that the poor village children given vouchers for private schools performed no better than those left behind in the government schools, although there was some consolation that the private schools achieved this result for a third of the cost of the government schools. However, investigating closely, I discovered that different tests in mathematics and science had been used for children in the public and some of the private schools, with questions posed in English for half of the private schools, but in Telugu, the regional language, in public schools. This violated a fundamental principle of randomized controlled trials—that everything should be the same apart from the intervention tested (in this case, the voucher)—and so invalidated the results.

However, tucked away in the research paper was evidence that when children were given the same tests, and when the Telugu-medium private schools were compared with the Telugu-medium public schools, the private school children significantly outperformed those in government schools in all subjects. Not only were the private schools more cost-effective, they also had higher achievement.[42]

I'm pleased that I managed to share these last findings with Andrew Coulson before he died. Moving forward, I regret I've lost a magnificent friend and sounding board to continue to engage in the debate, as further criticisms of market education will inevitably emerge.

7. Measure Market Presence, or Few Rules and Provider Neutrality: Are the Differences Important?

John Merrifield

Andrew Coulson and I agreed on the need to increase openness to alternatives to assigned public schools, the need for increased freedom from regulation for education consumers and school operators, and the need for market-based prices to inform and motivate schooling consumers and providers. Central planning has never worked, anywhere, economywide or industrywide. Market-driven price change orchestrates decentralized planning. Moreover, we agreed on the importance of truth in labeling, and that if we could start from scratch, it would be best if nonrefundable tuition tax credits were the only government intervention in the formal schooling industry.

Alas, since school system reform can't start from scratch, we often disagreed, which was both frustrating and productive. I believed that our strong differences of opinion were an important reason to define joint projects. You can learn a lot more from honest, well-meaning, well-informed disagreement than from people with mostly similar worldviews. I knew that Coulson was not an ideologue or paid political hack defending a position out of institutional or personal self-interest. Our disagreements on policy tactics were based on principle, not pique. He wanted the best outcome for our country, and for schoolchildren everywhere. I knew that he would provide a stern test of my ideas and interpretations of evidence. So, we had a war of ideas, and I proposed some coauthorships. I learned a lot from jousting with Andrew Coulson.

A discussion of our disagreements has value in its own right, because it bears on the crucial tactical choices school system reformers must make. And specifying the substantive bases of our disagreements has value in this tribute volume because Coulson and I tussled over core issues that deserve a lot more scholarly attention. Those general tactical disagreements set the table for our disagreement on how to measure the likely key underlying conditions of high performing school systems that is the main subject of this chapter.

After starting with a focus on how to create an Education Freedom Index (EFI), Coulson developed two versions of what became the Cato Education Market Index (CEMI). I continued to pursue the EFI concept: a measurement of freedom from constraint without regard to the nature of the choices made. I will get to the EFI vs. CEMI tussles, and the specifics of the key differences. But first I want to set the scene with our overarching discussion of how best to pursue a transformation from our current, centrally planned, gold-plated, school system disaster, to a high-performing, relentlessly improving system, with all of the schooling options, public and private.

Sufficiency of Nonrefundable Tuition Tax Credits

Coulson and I agreed that nonrefundable tuition tax credits are an appropriate government intervention in the formal schooling industry, but we did not agree on how to get there. To Coulson, the answer was obvious: implement a nonrefundable tuition tax credit in every school system, which in the United States would mean in every state. I said that would be fine, but it would not be transformational given our starting point—specifically the presence of a public school system offering tuition-free schooling funded at the cost of over $13,000 per pupil, per year. A nonrefundable credit would not defray tuition costs very much for most households, even those with only one school-age child, so a nonrefundable credit would not appreciably erode the school finance monopoly that makes it so difficult for a private school to compete. A nonrefundable tuition tax credit would not greatly increase the demand for private schooling, and thus it would not adequately create new schooling options or increase competition from new private schools. I argued that the tuition tax credit for most households would be too small to be a catalyst for school system transformation.

I concluded that tuition tax credits would be insufficient given my assumptions about the limits that would arise from the traditional tax liability base for credits, generally, and from thinking about where immediate fiscal savings would accrue when children left their assigned public schools. The maximum nonrefundable tax credit amount would vary by state, with the smallest and thus least transformational presumably in the lowest tax states. Some states have low property taxes, and some have no state income tax. Except for high-income households in high-income-tax states or high-property-tax states, even a 100 percent refund of the current state and local tax liability would provide only a partial tuition discount for one enrolled child. A nonrefundable tuition tax credit is nearly meaningless to low-income, and hence low-tax-liability, households.

Coulson had answers.[1]

The first was to extend nonrefundable tax credits to businesses and households without schoolchildren for donating money to organizations that fund tuition vouchers for low-income families. On the need for such donation credits, Coulson and I were in complete agreement. Meaningful tuition tax credits would not be appropriate or politically feasible without the donation tax credit complementarity. Many states now offer such a nonrefundable tax credit mix as tax credit scholarships (TCS), though the term "scholarship" is misleading. TCS-based tuition grants are not restricted to children with superior academic skills. More important, TCS programs help many families afford options than aren't available in the public school system. But scholarships have been too scarce, and amounts too small, to be transformational. They have been unable to attract significantly increased investment in private schools.

The second answer was a proposal to include multiple state and local taxes in the liability basis for the nonrefundable tax credits: the property tax revenue of school districts plus state income and sales tax, and perhaps other state and local taxes. But even with the addition of credits based on seemingly unlikely nonschool local government (such as city or county) taxes, the possible annual nonrefundable credit was still well below the tuition levels of many private school options.

The struggle to adequately fund school choice from credits against current state and local tax liabilities exists because households directly pay only part of the taxes that finance the public school system. They also indirectly pay through school taxes on businesses. And the taxes that households directly pay, they pay their entire lives, not just when their children are in school, which is when they would be eligible for the nonrefundable tuition tax credit Coulson proposed. Credits against the taxes families pay to finance the public school system just while their children are in school can yield only a small fraction of the total tuition cost. I'm slow sometimes, so it took me several years—obviously too late—to propose to Coulson that we fully flesh out how one might enlarge the ultimate credit amount by tuition tax credit banking. Thus, for example, a taxpayer/parent who spends $5,000 per year on tuition for 10 years could earn a $2,000 nonrefundable credit for 25 years, with many of those years coming after the child has left school.

Public school finance is an implicit loan that families repay through continued school tax payments after their children are out of a school. A bankable tuition tax credit would do the opposite. Families would provide the funding up front, perhaps through a real loan, and then get repaid with lower taxes later on. I said that I was sure that the possible annual tuition tax credit of most households would be too small to be a catalyst for school system transformation. With tuition tax credit banking, I believe the credit can be large enough to be transformational.

The Regulation-Following-Money Threat

The degree to which regulation of content and practices would follow government money is a key part of the tuition tax credit debate and central to credible measurement of educational freedom. Coulson had an encyclopedic knowledge of the many instances in which increased government control of nongovernment schooling options followed the introduction of government funding of such schools. He was also well versed in the court cases ruling that vouchers and refundable tax credits amount to government funding, while nonrefundable credits do not. The courts see nonrefundable tax credits as giving taxpayers back their own money, but they often view vouchers and refundable credits as giving private—including religious—schools taxpayer money. Still, there is considerable disagreement on how much government control of schooling practices would follow different means of leveling the financial playing field between public and private schooling options.

Government control does not follow many kinds of government funding, and the government can already regulate private schools. But Coulson was adamant that government—the political process—was much more likely to refrain from debilitating regulation of private schools if there were no taxpayer dollars to spur calls for "accountability." To secure that reduced regulation risk through nonrefundable tax credits only, most families in most states would still face huge out-of-pocket tuition costs, which would keep many from opting for an alternative to their assigned public school.

If bankable, nonrefundable tuition tax credits are not politically feasible, or still not large enough to induce transformational entrepreneurial initiative, I'm willing to forsake the smaller regulation risk of nonrefundable credits, vouchers for education savings accounts that foster greater choice and increased market entry by entrepreneurs. Coulson was not willing to forsake nonrefundable credits' smaller regulation risk. I suggested that we make an effort to measure the differences in regulation risk or, more generally, the resulting differences in the level of education freedom and conduciveness to a competitive school marketplace. A study of the determinants of education freedom, generally, and regulation of schooling content and practices, in particular, would have to wait until we had a measure of market openness to education entrepreneurship, and the degree to which public and private school operators were free from regulatory constraint. Enter the EFI.

Freedom of Choice

We started out with the name, Education Freedom Index (EFI), for what we expected to measure. From the start, we disagreed on what should be measured or valued in the 0–100 index. That led us to work independently and then return to discuss differences around a large Cato conference table. Coulson and I assertively exchanged ideas. We must have overwhelmed everyone else. On many key issues, no one else added their thoughts. The index name changed at the conference table when I noted that Coulson's template directly measured how much of formal schooling at the primary and secondary level—K–12—was produced privately, through markets. I argued that the result of Andrew's survey questions and calculations could not be called an EFI because the proposed calculations would value some choices more than others; an EFI should be neutral as to how families used their freedom. The EFI should not be larger when families have a lower propensity to choose public schools. Freedom from constraint would likely lead to increased reliance on markets to determine what kinds of instructional approaches to make available, where, how they would be produced, and for whom. But I believed the index should directly measure freedom from constraint and government neutrality about the provider, not the likely outcomes of freedom and a level playing field between public and private providers. For example, the school choice expansions created by mostly narrowly targeted programs, so far, have largely seen the vast majority of families choosing their assigned public school. Exactly how many of the program-eligible children stay in their assigned public school affects the CEMI value, but not the EFI value.

So, I argued, if a policy change significantly lowers the cost of moving a child from the assigned public school to a private alternative, a low number of transfers to the private alternative should not reflect negatively in a true EFI. If an index did penalize opting for the assigned public school, it should be called an education market index (EMI). Coulson agreed, adding a "C" for Cato (CEMI). I also pointed out that appropriate reforms would take many years to turn the status quo into full-fledged markets; Coulson developed a "policy-rating" version of the CEMI to measure the extent to which a new or proposed policy would create the conditions that would support full-fledged markets for formal schooling options. My EFI is most similar to the "policy-rating" CEMI, but significant differences remain.

To his great credit, Coulson set the scene for the specific disagreements. He stated a well-developed case for his policy and measurement protocol preferences, for example, in his book *Market Education: The Unknown History*.[2] I critiqued some of the *Market Education*–based interpretations. Then, mostly on the basis of my book *The School Choice Wars* and my Edgewood Voucher Program assessment, I offered different interpretations—which Coulson nearly always rejected.[3] Likewise, he was first with an extensive, brilliant measurement template. His survey questions were the starting point for the mostly similar, sometimes identical, 49 survey questions in the original EFI. Later, to spur data entry activity, I condensed the original 49-question EFI template down to the current 16 questions. Because of his leadership, I am naming the online EFI calculator the "Andrew Coulson Education Freedom Index."[4] As the developer of nearly all of the key starting points for revision and fine-tuning, he deserves the honor. I recognize, however, that since the EFI concept was not Coulson's first preference for the underlying concepts, the name change might send him spinning in his grave. To guard against that, and for solid scholarly reasons, I hope we can do some extensive EFI–CEMI empirical comparisons, such as examining explanatory variables for key effects like academic outcomes and rate of school system change.

Index Specifics—EFI vs. CEMI—Similarities and Differences

The aim of this section is to highlight key differences between the two indexes. The computational and conceptual details are in the publications that describe the EFI and CEMI.[5] How the computational strategy aggregates the component scores into an index number between 0 and 100 is one of the key differences. The CEMI value results from multiplying the producer and consumer freedom scores, which are themselves the products of individual producer and consumer freedom components:

CEMI = Competitive Density * Incentives for Innovation and Expansion * Incentive for Efficiency * Entry and Operational Freedom * Incentive for Parental Responsibility * Parental Freedom of Choice * 100

Multiplication of scores means that any low score, especially a zero, makes the other factors meaningless. As a conceptual matter, that multiplicative aggregation strategy is clearly appropriate for some school system features, such as "entry and operational freedom," which includes the barriers to private school start-up and regulation of schooling personnel and content. Certainly, other high scores are virtually irrelevant to market functionality if the "entry and operational freedom" value is low.

But many of the other CEMI components can be low without coming close to extinguishing freedom or substantially curbing market activity. That is, low scores for some of the factors in the CEMI equation should not zero out a measure of market activity. For example, a universal tuition voucher amount, or an annual education savings account deposit, close to the average tuition cost of private schools would zero out "Incentive for Efficiency" and "Incentive for Parental Responsibility," and thus yield a zero CEMI. That result occurs in the computation of the CEMI even though "subsidies to private schools can also have a separate, positive impact on market vigor if they increase competition between public and private schools by diminishing any existing subsidy discrimination that favors the government-run schools."[6]

As Coulson found in the research that yielded *Market Education*, school systems perform better when parents have some "skin in the game"—when there is a substantial out-of-pocket cost associated with a school choice. But the multiplicative aggregation of components with unequal importance exaggerates the importance of skin in the game and other important, but not critical, factors.

The EFI summary value between 0 and 100 arises from the addition of component values. Since each component is clearly not equally important, the EFI directly addresses the weighting uncertainty problem (unknown W1 to W8) that many other indices ignore by implicitly assuming equal weights.

$$EFI = (W1 * EBS) + (W2 * PDI) + (W3 * APC) + (W4 * MSTAB) + (W5 * FTM) + (W6 * MREG) + (W7 * OPC) + (W8 * PAIS)$$

My journal article on the EFI describes several ways of dealing with weighting uncertainty, including deriving the EFI value for all possible combinations of all credible weights, and then publishing the minimum, maximum, and average EFI value derived from that process.[7] The online EFI calculator derives two of those.[8] The first is weighting based on my judgment, which means the following weights: 24 percent (W1) for formal and informal factors that would undermine entrepreneurial initiative (EBS: entry barriers); 24 percent (W2) for factors that would limit product differentiation (PDI: for example, rules requiring particular textbooks or the same curriculum elements everywhere); 20 percent (W3) for absence of price control (APC); 16 percent (W4) for market stability (MSTAB: degree of legislative or legal jeopardy); and 4 percent each (W5 to W8) for freedom through mobility (FTM), miscellaneous regulation (MREG: not schooling content or personnel), out-of-pocket cost (OPC), and parent information system (PAIS). The second thing the EFI calculator derives is reconfigured components to create a credible equal weights scenario.

The EFI takes account of constraints on the potential to earn a profit, but not the extent of actual profit seeking. The CEMI varies with the enrollment of schools aiming to earn a profit. The fully adjusted EFI takes account of the rarely recognized toxic combination of price control and potential profit. That combination creates a "negative freedom" that is evident, but not widely recognized, in U.S. chartered public schools. Because chartered public schools suffer price control (zero price for customers and whatever the state formula specifies for the school operators), shortages are widespread and large—a situation that empowers school operators to cut corners, often scandalously, to increase profit or revenue available for additional disbursements. Quality reduction is a well-established outcome of the persistent shortages (widespread, long waitlists) that result from price caps below the market-clearing level. When the resulting unhappy customers leave the school, they are readily replaced from the waitlist. Quality reduction is a tempting producer response to persistent shortages because, up to a point, cutting corners reduces costs, but not revenues.

The EFI's out-of-pocket-cost (OPC) component addresses the parental skin-in-the-game issue. OPC addresses the schooling access versus parental responsibility tradeoff created by changes in the out-of-pocket cost of schooling. This includes costs like tuition due on top of taxes (for some private schools) that must be paid regardless of school usage or the school chosen. Pending a research effort to measure that tradeoff, I specified 50 percent as the freedom-maximizing out-of-pocket cost. That means the EFI implicitly assumes that an OPC change from 0 to 50 percent improves parental responsibility via more family skin in the game, and outweighs increased financial stress from increased out-of-pocket costs, increasing overall freedom. From 50 to 100 percent OPC (no subsidy), the effect of less access to private schooling dominates the effects of further increases in skin in the game. Obviously, on the basis of my "best guess" weight of 4 percent, and Coulson's willingness to zero out the CEMI on the basis of minimal parental skin in the game, that treatment of parental out-of-pocket cost is a major CEMI–EFI difference. I'd argue that even with no skin in the game, many parents would still very carefully choose a school for their children, and relatively small percentages of careful choosers are sufficient to foster a high level of market competitiveness, including careful attention to the nature of consumer preferences.

The EFI addresses the criticality of low barriers to entrepreneurial initiative by also using the entry barrier score, which directly accounts for 24 percent of the EFI value, as a weight for scoring anything pertaining to private schools. For example, price control only has its full W3 value (best guess = 20 percent) if there are no formal or informal barriers to entrepreneurial initiative. In other words, absence of price control does not increase the EFI value much if huge difficulties sustaining a private school (e.g., onerous regulation of registration requirements or a public-school, public-finance monopoly) severely discourage entrepreneurial initiative. Likewise, minimal regulation of private school materials, personnel, and curriculum does not create much useful freedom if the public school finance monopoly amounts to a huge private school entry barrier.

EFI's measure of market stability (MSTAB) is another key EFI–CEMI difference. A stable basis for market activity is a clear prerequisite of producer freedom. In general, the rule of law provides that stability. Potential entrepreneurs come forward when they know that the courts will enforce their contracts. In the context of school system change, perceived stability exists when laws provide, for example, a more level playing field between public and private schools. That would include laws establishing universal vouchers or tuition tax credits or education savings accounts with annual values near the per-pupil funding level of public schools if those laws seem likely to survive legal challenges and attempts at legislative repeal. Uncertainty will proportionately curb entrepreneurial initiative.

Summary and Concluding Remarks

Andrew Coulson was a brilliant man and a passionate scholar. We agreed on the big things but often bumped heads on tactics and analytical methods. Ultimately, that creative tension will turn out to be much more important than if we had agreed. With his terribly premature loss, the world may never realize the school system reform so desperately needed nearly everywhere. I hope that the rest of us can benefit from his considerable contributions to the discovery of critical facts and his work to develop productive ways to interpret them, and we can adequately move the debate forward without him. It'll be tough.

The two areas on which I worked with Coulson will likely be critical to how and whether we achieve productive school system reforms in enough locations that they eventually spread to the places most hostile to such reform. The first is determining the appropriate policy vehicle for eroding the public school system's public finance monopoly, and thus substantially leveling the playing field between the government-run schools and truly independent schools. A bad choice might result in an outcome worse than smaller academic and economic gains. It could cause abandonment of productive pathways to school system reform.

The second is the measurement of market presence—or freedom—in formal schooling for children. Coulson provided the basis for his focus on market presence through the CEMI, and for my focus on the presence of freedom, regardless of the degree to which increased freedom leads to increased market accountability in the provision of formal schooling to children. We need a CEMI or EFI to establish the importance of market presence, and maybe freedom, to school system effectiveness and related economic and political outcomes. We may need both.

8. Toward Education Consistent with Freedom

Neal P. McCluskey

If you were to start an education system from scratch for a pluralist country dedicated to liberty, would you likely determine that the government should run the schools and decide what all children will learn? Probably not. Yet that is exactly what the United States has done, along with numerous other countries ostensibly committed to freedom. Indeed, many no doubt well-intentioned education thinkers have asserted that such a system is essential to a free society.

Andrew Coulson knew better and attacked such thinking head-on. Coulson fought for school choice—the only education system truly compatible with liberty and peace—to maximize freedom not just for students, but for all Americans. As much as test scores, efficient spending, taking quality to scale, and all the other things education reformers obsess over, liberty was essential to Coulson.

Public schooling defenders often say that public schooling—government schooling—is an indispensable American institution, as if it were a God-given fact, especially when they perceive threats from school choice. When Betsy DeVos, a committed backer of choice, was nominated to be President Donald Trump's secretary of education, American Federation of Teachers president Randi Weingarten attacked her in a *New York Daily News* op-ed as a "grave threat to what made America great": public schools. Weingarten rhapsodized that public schools are "the places where we prepare the nation's young people—rich, poor, native- and foreign-born, and of all abilities—to contribute. They are where we forge a common culture out of America's rich diversity."[1] Political theorist Benjamin Barber has pronounced that public schools are the "institutions where we learn what it means to be a public and start down the road toward common national and civic identity. They are the forges of our citizenship and the bedrock of our democracy."[2]

Modern apologists for public schooling are not alone in arguing that government-run schools are essential to molding unum from pluribus.

Forging unity was the primary intention of leading advocates of public schooling from the earliest days of the republic. Benjamin Rush, surgeon general of the Continental Army and a leading light in Pennsylvania, was a powerful voice calling out for public schooling to unify diverse Americans. He did not sugarcoat his goal, writing, "Our schools of learning, by producing one general and uniform system of education, will render the mass of the people more homogeneous and thereby fit them more easily for uniform and peaceable government."[3] Similarly, Horace Mann, the first secretary of the Massachusetts Board of Education and the "Father of the Common School," wrote that in the public schools "the affinities of a common nature should unite them [children] together so as to give the advantages of pre-occupancy and a stable possession of fraternal feelings, against the alienating competitions of subsequent life."[4]

Some evidence suggests that Americans broadly feel that public schooling is a necessary, unifying institution. In 2001, political scientist Terry Moe detected what he called a "public school ideology . . . a normative attachment to the public schools."[5] The basis for his conclusion was three survey questions he posed to the general public and also to parents of school-aged children. Perhaps most directly telling was the response to the statement, "The more children attend public schools, rather than private or parochial schools, the better it is for American society." Some 41 percent of nonparents agreed with this—a large chunk of Americans—as did 40 percent of parents with children in only public schools, and more than a quarter of parents who used both public and private schools, or even exclusively private schools!

What if the public schools were not working well? Apparently, for the vast majority of Americans, even that would not matter: 67 percent of nonparent respondents agreed that "the public schools deserve our support even if they are performing poorly." Note that bad public schools are not just legally entitled to support. No, they also "deserve" it. Such deep support may well stem from a belief—perhaps just a gut feeling—that public schools are essential unifiers.

The problem is that the public schools are not unifiers. They may, in fact, be net dividers. Noting the wide range of education before public schooling, Coulson explained in his book, *Market Education: The Unknown History*, that fearing "balkanization" in the absence of public schooling gets the causal effect of force "exactly backwards": it is requiring all people to support a single schooling provider, not educational freedom, that ignites conflict and sows division:

> Prior to the government's involvement in education, there were nondenominational schools, Quaker schools and Lutheran schools, fundamentalist schools and more liberal Protestant schools, classical schools and technical schools, in accordance with the preferences of local communities. Some had homogeneous enrollments; others drew students from across ethnic and religious lines. In areas where schools of different sects coexisted, they and their patrons seldom came into conflict, because they did not try to foist their views on one another. They lived and let live in what were comparatively stable, though increasingly diverse, communities. It was only after the state began creating uniform institutions for all children that these families were thrown into conflict. Within public schools, many parents were faced with an unpleasant choice: accept that objectionable ideas would be forced on their children, or force their own ideas on everyone else's children by taking control of the system. It was this artificial choice between two evils that led to the Philadelphia Bible Riots, the beatings of Catholic children, the denigration of immigrant values and lifestyles in public schools and textbooks, and laws—which today would be viewed as utterly unconstitutional—forcing the Protestant Bible on all families. The unpardonable treatment of black families by the government schools, which persisted for over a century, does nothing to enlighten this grim picture.[6]

Democratically controlled schooling, which is understood to mean government-owned-and-operated education in which "the people" decide what the schools will teach, is inherently conflictual and unequal. Barring unanimity of thought among all people of a district, state, or nation—depending on which level of government is making the decisions—conflict is inevitable. You cannot teach both evolution and creationism as true, or simultaneously mandate and make truly voluntary the reading of Mark Twain's *Adventures of Huckleberry Finn* or Toni Morrison's *Beloved*. One side has to win, and the other lose. The result of this zero-sum game, as we've seen repeatedly, is social and political fisticuffs.[7]

Such conflict is typically resolved in one of two, ultimately unacceptable, ways: inequality under the law, or hollowed-out curricula.

When evolutionists keep creationism out of science classes, or a public school requires that students read about ol' Huck Finn while keeping

Beloved off of reading lists—when government chooses, as it must when creating curricula, to elevate some people's speech and downgrade others'—then one side is inherently rendered superior under the law, and one inferior. We have tyranny of the majority, or of a politically powerful minority. We have inequality.

Perhaps less offensive to bedrock American values is the second outcome: sidestepping potentially controversial topics. That option may avoid or defuse social conflict, but as researchers such as Diane Ravitch and political scientists Michael Berkman and Eric Plutzer have demonstrated, the result is education stripped of meaningful, rigorous content and engaging material. Government in that case may treat everyone equally, but for students, that means equally badly.[8]

Lest one take the conflict-and-inequality story too far, it is important to note that for much of American history, public schools and districts were generally not powder kegs just one inflammatory basal reader away from exploding. But that was because public schooling reality was miles away from the melting pot magic ascribed to it by backers. For most of American history, people tended to live in small, homogeneous communities, and it was in those decidedly un-pluralist places that schooling decisions were made. And when there was heterogeneity? As historian Benjamin Justice found when poring over records from 19th-century New York, differing groups often created separate districts or schools.[9]

Then there was what Coulson referred to at the end of the quotation earlier in this chapter: the supposedly unifying public schools disgracefully excluded African Americans, and when blacks were finally allowed to use the system, they were cordoned off in segregated schools, even in such "enlightened" places as Boston, Massachusetts.[10] And African Americans were not the only racial or ethnic group shunted either de jure or de facto into isolated schools: in some parts of the country, people of Mexican or Asian heritage were confined to their own "separate but equal" public institutions.

Choice Is Freedom, Minimized Compulsion Is More Freedom

If we wish to end schooling-driven social conflict and inequality, we must open the gates of the gladiatorial arena in which Americans are forced to fight. Rather than requiring everyone to fund public schools, money should be attached to students and educators allowed to start and run schools as they see fit. As Coulson wrote in *Market Education,*

> When it comes to serving the needs of individual families, the case for the superiority of educational markets over government monopolies is a strong one. Even some diehard advocates of public schooling are willing to admit it. What prevents them from throwing their support behind choice is not the fear that parents will fail to get the kinds of schools they want, but that they will succeed. A great diversity of schools would spring up under a system of unhindered educational freedom, and supporters of government schooling worry that such diversity would lead to social discord and balkanization. While these concerns stem from the best intentions, it is difficult not to be shocked by their bald and bitter irony . . .
>
> It is not the patrons of private Atheist Academies and Evangelical Elementaries who tear into one another on the subject of evolution versus creation. It is not the private Afrocentric school, or Orthodox Jewish school, or Classical Western Culture school that sows dissension among families in the neighborhood. It was not the private Catholic primary school of nineteenth-century America that drove its community into a frenzy by foisting its version of the Bible on all the local children. It was, however, the state schools of post-revolutionary France that set citizen against citizen by favoring republican or royalist views according to the whim of despots; and it is the modern U.S. public school system that factionalizes the population on issues of curriculum and religion, eating away at the fabric of the nation year after year like the relentless action of waves eroding what could be a peaceful shore.[11]

That choice would allow Americans to live more peacefully is difficult to refute, though one school of thought holds that the conflict inherent in public schooling is a feature, not a bug, forcing people to learn to work out their differences.[12] This is mistaken. Not only is winner-take-all conflict divisive by its nature, but also history is clear that immigrants—the primary "other" that public schools have been intended to assimilate—will adjust to and adopt broad American culture and values on their own, because doing so is the key to succeeding. People are simply more comfortable, and better able to earn a living, when they can speak the common language, and when they adopt shared American culture. When this assimilation happens at the individual and family level, it can occur at a rate that is gradual—not shocking and destructive—allowing people to slowly take on the new while preserving what they most value of the old.[13] When government tries to impose it, in contrast, the result is not just conflict but fracturing of families—the younger generation is taught to reject the values and culture of their parents—and sometimes bitter resentment.[14]

That said, there is another important objection to choice, and it is consistent with the reason for backing choice: some forms of choice compel support of ideas and beliefs that some—maybe most—taxpayers may find troubling, even abhorrent. Preventing such compulsion is the justification for the many "Blaine" amendments and "compelled support" clauses in state constitutions that have sometimes thwarted choice programs.

Blaine amendments have their roots in sometimes bigoted 19th-century politics targeting Roman Catholics: Sen. James G. Blaine (R-ME) wanted no public funding ever to go to Catholic schools trying to survive against Protestant public institutions. Nonetheless, in theory, they can serve a laudable goal. As Thomas Jefferson warned in the Virginia Statute for Religious Freedom, "To compel a man to furnish contributions of money for the propagation of opinions which he disbelieves and abhors, is sinful and tyrannical."[15] Blaine amendments stand against such compulsion, at least when it comes to subsidizing religious institutions, though by blocking funding only to religious institutions they ultimately discriminate against religion.

To be clear, freedom would be greatly expanded were, say, all children to receive vouchers in the amount of their share of public schooling dollars and educators were freed to create schools and other educational arrangements according to their own pedagogical, moral, or other ideals. Parents could seek out schools with democratic control by students, or Baptist schools, or classical academies, or classical Baptist academies with democratic control by students. Educators offering different models could freely choose to work with parents seeking them. But the use of vouchers compels any taxpayer opposed to any of those options to supply funds to propagate opinions or beliefs to which he objects.

Coulson had a solution to the very real, bedrock worry about unjust compulsion, one that created tension in the voucher-centric choice community when he advanced it: tax credits for individuals or corporations that donate to groups providing private school scholarships. Reminding readers in his report, "Forging Consensus," that "compulsion has been the single greatest source of education-related social conflict in history," Coulson stated that no matter the sordid, anti-Catholic lineage of Blaine amendments, "voucher programs force some citizens to violate their convictions." Then he asked the crucial moral question: "Is it right to increase parents' freedom of choice at the expense of taxpayers' freedom of conscience?"[16] His answer: absolutely not.

How do tax credits avoid that moral violation? With credits, no taxpayer sends money to the state, which then forwards it to parents to choose schools. With personal use credits—which taxpayers receive to offset the cost of private schooling for their own children—individuals can freely choose a private school and are, essentially, relieved from paying twice for education.

Donation credits are only a bit more complicated. Corporations or individuals who donate to nonprofit groups that furnish private schooling scholarships receive credits on their taxes for some portion—preferably all—of their donations. Again, what is essentially happening is that donors are getting credits for spending money on scholarships that would otherwise have been used for government schools. Crucially, though, people get to choose whether to donate, and, ideally, to what kinds of schools: Roman Catholic, nondenominational Christian, Montessori, and so on. Vouchers may enhance the freedom of students and their families, but tax credit scholarships also enhance the freedom of taxpayers.

For defense of liberty—the fundamental American value—the best possible government role is to provide tax credits for those who fund private school choices. Tax credits also seem to be a more effective way to expand choice than vouchers. As of the beginning of 2016, just shy of 400,000 children were using either vouchers, tax credit–eligible scholarships, or education savings accounts (ESAs) to attend private schools. Of those choice vehicles, vouchers started much earlier than tax credits, but only 166,579 students were using them; 225,834 had credit-eligible scholarships, and 6,867 were recipients of ESAs.[17]

Not only are tax credits more consistent with liberty and much faster growing than vouchers, Coulson found empirically that they are also less prone to regulation.[18] Likely in large part because they involve no government funding, the impetus to attach regulations to scholarships is not as strong as under vouchers. No taxpayer's money is being used at Bob Jones Elementary, or Ayn Rand High School, or even just a school with low test scores. Schools attended by students using tax credit–eligible scholarships simply do not receive state funds.

Of course, even tax credits are connected to government. Giving credits for schooling and not, say, buying ultra high-definition televisions, puts the government's thumb on the scale for education. But the tax credit is by far the least coercive approach to help make true educational freedom possible. That is except, perhaps, for tax credit–eligible donations to ESAs. ESA programs typically authorize state governments to put money into accounts for individual children that can then be used for education. ESAs expand on the freedom of vouchers and scholarships by enabling parents not just to pick schools, but also to purchase individual courses, buy equipment for homeschooling, save for college, or apply the funds to other educational uses.

ESAs by their nature produce more freedom than vouchers, enabling parents to customize their children's learning far beyond just choosing a school. But they suffer from the same basic state funding problem as vouchers: government gives Peter's money to Paul. As a result, even though he was battling cancer at the time, Coulson was a big part of Cato's work formulating tax credits for ESA donations. The resulting paper—"Taking Credit for Education: How to Fund Education Savings Accounts through Tax Credits"—was authored by Jason Bedrick, Jonathan Butcher, and Clint Bolick and published in January 2016, one month before Coulson's death.[19] With its paramount focus on liberty, it is a leading edge of Coulson's educational freedom legacy.

Conclusion

The school choice debate—indeed, all education debates—seems to quickly be reduced to simplistic questions of test scores or spending levels—easy measures of immediate costs and narrow benefits. But much deeper, and much more central to the role of schooling in a free society, is how the education system brings us together . . . or pulls us apart. Does it foster social cohesion while upholding the basic tenets of American life: liberty, and equality under the law? Or does it do the opposite? Alas, these questions are far too infrequently asked.

Perhaps the reason for the relative silence is a pervasive, unchallenged, and ultimately unsupported assumption: that pushing all diverse people into a single, government school system will make everyone get along and unify the country. It was an assumption that Andrew Coulson rejected, both because he knew it was not grounded in historical reality and because forced uniformity is a notion fundamentally incompatible with a harmonious and free society. "Democratic" public schooling by its very nature produces winners and losers, which is utterly antithetical to equality under the law and inescapably incites peace-destroying social conflict.

School choice is the key to escaping this most—let's be frank—un-American of education systems. Choice ends the high stakes, zero-sum game by ensuring that the public can get educated without the most politically powerful segment of society deciding for everyone else what their children will—or will not—learn in the schools for which all must pay. Andrew Coulson knew that choice is key. He also knew that how choice is delivered matters immensely, and that vouchers—even if a vast improvement over the status quo—still involve coercion and violate freedom of conscience. So he championed a form of choice with the greatest attendant freedom—tax credits for scholarship donations—and in the process advanced the choice vehicle that has, to date, brought educational freedom to the most children. Andrew showed that the principled and the practical—the most freedom for all, and the most choice for families—go together. He championed the best way to deliver education in a country founded on liberty.

Testimonials

When Andrew Coulson passed away, numerous people from the education policy world wrote pieces remembering him and his work. We reproduce several of those testimonials here, with apologies for any we missed.

Neal McCluskey and Jason Bedrick

Director (McCluskey) and then-policy analyst (Bedrick), Center for Educational Freedom, Cato Institute

Early yesterday morning, after a 15-month battle with brain cancer, Senior Fellow in Education Policy Andrew Coulson passed away. He is survived by his beloved wife, Kay. Andrew was 48 years old.

Andrew's death is very sad news for everyone at Cato, but especially those of us at the Center for Educational Freedom, where Andrew was the director—and an almost impossibly sunny colleague—for more than a decade. Coming from a software engineering background, Andrew seized on education reform—and the need for educational freedom—not because he had spent a career in education, but because he saw a system that was illogical, that was hurting society and children, and that needed to be fixed.

And when Andrew wanted to fix something, he went to work.

Andrew hit the radars of everyone involved in education reform—especially school choice—with his 1999 book *Market Education: The Unknown History*, which captured exactly what he wanted everyone to know about education. For much of history, Andrew made clear, education was grounded in the free and voluntary interactions of teachers, students, and families—and it worked better for everyone than the rigid, moribund, government-dominated model we have today.

Andrew was in the reform vanguard not just in laying out the historical, logical, and empirical case for truly free-market education, but also in determining how, practically, to do that. Andrew was perhaps the earliest and clearest voice calling for tax credit–funded choice in preference to publicly funded voucher programs, which are themselves infinitely preferable to being assigned to a school based simply on your home address. Tax credit programs, he argued, would be more attractive—except to those who would lard regulations onto schools—by breaking the connection between state money and school choices. People would choose whether to donate to scholarships, and even to which organizations or schools such donations would go, rather than have the state hand out funds from all taxpayers.

Today, the wisdom of this choice mechanism has been borne out, with tax credit–based programs starting later than vouchers, but now exceeding total enrollment by about 53,000 students. And enrollment through private educational choice programs of all types—vouchers, tax credits, and education savings accounts—has ballooned since 1999, when *Market Education* was published, from just a few thousand children to nearly 400,000.

That is tremendous progress. But as Andrew would be the first to proclaim, it is not nearly enough. Indeed, with an eye to pushing choice much further, before he died, Andrew was putting the finishing touches on a documentary series vividly and humorously illustrating why we need educational freedom, and the great benefits that even limited freedom in education has produced. We hope Andrew's labor of love will be appearing on television sets across the country in the coming months.

Andrew Coulson is no longer with us. Thankfully, his ideas remain, and they will always illuminate the pathway forward.

Originally appeared at Cato-at-Liberty

Adam B. Schaeffer

Founder, Evolving Strategies, and former policy analyst, Center for Educational Freedom, Cato Institute

Andrew J. Coulson was my friend and mentor in school choice policy. He was a good, principled, brilliant, and funny man whom I will miss deeply, along with many, many others. Andrew was so much more than his work, but I'd like to focus here on that legacy he leaves behind, for those who never had the pleasure of knowing him personally.

There is no one else besides Andrew Coulson that you must read to discover what reforms we need in education and why they will work. That is not hyperbole. There are many very sharp people who have contributed important thoughts on education reform, but you will get everything essential that you need from reading through Andrew's collective works. In the near future, his final project—a documentary series on the history and future of education—will be released and should be added as mandatory viewing.

All the way through Andrew's illness, he continued work on his passion: bringing freedom and excellence to education and opportunities to children. I know he has made a huge difference already, but I hope even more people read and learn from Andrew after his passing. If you have even a fleeting interest in education reform, do yourself a favor and read as much as you can by Andrew Coulson.

I was first introduced to Andrew in graduate school, about 12 years ago. I'd written an article for National Review Online on vouchers, playing off a *West Wing* episode to encourage conservatives and Republicans to provoke a wedge-issue fight for targeted vouchers and black voters. Someone working in the choice movement emailed to compliment me on the article, but gently suggested I might be missing some important concerns about school choice policy.

He attached a late draft of a paper written by Andrew for the Mackinac Center called "Forging Consensus." I read it. And that was it. I was convinced that education tax credits are the best option for remaking our education system into one of freedom and excellence, one where we can provide the best opportunities possible to all children. In terms of practical impact, principle, public opinion, politics, and legal restrictions, Andrew made a thoroughly convincing case for consensus on what the goals of school choice proponents should be.

More than a decade later, I'm more convinced than ever that Andrew was correct then and is still correct now. His work directly inspired my PhD dissertation, and I ultimately went to work for Andrew at the Cato Institute. I don't think it's an exaggeration to say that everything I've written on education reform since then has been a recapitulation or an extension of Andrew's thinking and analysis.

Andrew was a fine thinker and passionate advocate. But, as many have noted, he was also a kind man with a splendid sense of humor and relentless optimism. He remained immovably committed to his principles and the conclusions to which his great mind had led him. But he always engaged with a sense of magnanimity and humor, never bitterness or anger. Even when I made a good deal of trouble for him with my lack of these qualities, Andrew stood by me. When he faced difficulties because of his principles, he always stood firm on those as well.

I wish more of his qualities had rubbed off on me along with his ideas. I had a great deal of difficulty maintaining my balance and optimism to continue in what I knew would be an extraordinarily long and difficult battle. Andrew did not, or at least he never let it show or slow him down.

Andrew's passing is a great personal loss to those of us who knew and worked with him. It's an even greater loss to our collective movement to expand liberty and opportunity. But Andrew would never approve of ending on such a gloomy note. So I'll keep in mind all the wonderful gifts he's left us—the memories and impact of his friendship and the continuing inspiration and power of his ideas.

Originally appeared at Cato-at-Liberty

Lisa Snell

Director of education, Reason Foundation

I am so sad to hear of the passing of Andrew J. Coulson. It was my great fortune to work in education policy with Andrew toward a better education for all kids and to know he always held the line and set the pace for true markets in education. *Market Education: The Unknown History* is the book I tell everyone interested in education to start with!

Originally appeared on Lisa Snell's Facebook page

Thomas A. Shull

Adjunct scholar, Mackinac Center for Public Policy, and former senior editor and senior director of research quality

Yesterday saw the early death of the Mackinac Center's former senior fellow in education policy, Andrew Coulson. Andrew was the victim of brain cancer—a malignancy that he fought with all of the energy, intelligence, grace, and good humor that characterized his life and work.

Andrew's first profession was as a software engineer for Microsoft, where he worked on the seminal operating system Windows 95. His subsequent decision to enter the realm of education policy appears to have been as felicitous for him as it was for the rest of us—a step that allowed his vocation and avocation to become one.

I first learned of his groundbreaking research on the success of private markets in education from an unlikely source: the syndicated columnist William Raspberry. Raspberry was a political liberal who championed public schools, but who remained open-minded about their flaws. In a remarkable review of Andrew's book, *Market Education: The Unknown History*, Raspberry gave a serious hearing to a thesis most pundits would have rejected out of hand:

> Coulson's [*Market Education*] is a sweeping blow to those of us who keep hoping the system that served earlier generations reasonably well can be helped to overcome the effects of bad policies, inadequate teachers, disengaged parents, and indifferent students to perform its magic yet again. He wonders if the magic was ever there.

I recall my surprise as Raspberry seemed to grant the possibility that private schools might be an answer to the problem of better universal education, including education for the poor. At the time, this was a major concession, as I knew well. I was on the editorial board of the *Detroit News*, and my essays in defense of charter schools and public school choice were considered incendiary enough, despite both reforms' reliance on government institutions.

I became acquainted with Andrew in 2004 during my first few days at the Mackinac Center. As the center's new senior editor, I heard that the *Detroit Free Press* was questioning a figure in a column that Andrew, then the center's senior fellow in education, had written on the Detroit Public Schools. Knowing firsthand how treacherous DPS data could be, I called Andrew with some misgivings.

My apprehension quickly disappeared. Andrew was completely familiar with the federal data; he'd used it correctly; and he'd already responded to the *Free Press* with his source for the number. His relaxed and friendly answers revealed an easy competence that I was to encounter again and again in my work with him.

And what interesting work it was! Andrew wrote freely about the role of private education markets in helping the Dutch and the Japanese dominate world test scores, and the young people of India dominate American telephone help centers. He simply pummeled the argument that American students are outscored internationally because our schools are more democratic, and that our best and brightest compare well, even if our average students do not. He similarly dashed the notion that your local school was really pretty good, and that it was just those bad ones in the newspapers that dragged the U.S. average down.

Despite his religious agnosticism, he readily chronicled the superior record of Catholic schools in closing the academic achievement gap between different races of students. His even-handedness showed again when he profiled private K–12 scholarship institutions in Michigan, prominently listing the Children's Scholarship Fund, managed by the Catholic Archdiocese of Detroit. Indeed, he was able to discuss the hopelessly polarizing issue of religion and science in public schools while showing respect for all sides of the debate.

Andrew was even-handed in his goring of oxen, as well. For instance, while granting that charter schools had achieved some educational improvements, he forthrightly considered how charters helped push better-performing Catholic schools out of the market. Similarly, after leaving the [Mackinac] Center for the Washington, D.C.–based Cato Institute, he published research showing that the California charter schools that were most successful were not the ones growing and replicating.

Just as important, Andrew played a key role in forwarding the debate among free-marketers between tax credits and vouchers as vehicles for education reform. This was a sometimes pitched battle, yet he weathered it well and helped convince many in the movement of the superiority of tax credits—a stand the Mackinac Center championed early.

* * *

A key to all of this success was the unique temper of his commitment to reform. Instead of expressing the intensity of his passion in invective, Andrew channeled his passion into an unusual blend of productivity, hard research, humor, and intellectual joy. I suspect this is what Raspberry sensed in Andrew—a genuine goodwill that characterized Andrew's writing even as he was summarily proving you wrong.

And he was a delightful colleague. There was no one I enjoyed working with more than Andrew—a sentiment I suspect all his friends and coworkers share. I recall, too, James Tooley's words of gratitude in the foreword to his remarkable and path-breaking book *The Beautiful Tree: A Personal Journey into How the World's Poorest People Are Educating Themselves*. Andrew was the book's editor, and Tooley simply wrote, "Andrew Coulson has been the kind of editor and supporter an author dreams of, through good times and bad."

* * *

Perhaps most tellingly, Andrew's passion expressed itself in a willingness to learn. He stayed current with education research. He pressed himself to master complicated statistical skills, most notably in his conceptually vigorous Mackinac Center study "School District Consolidation, Size and Spending: An Evaluation." More recently, and almost until his death, he bootstrapped himself up the learning curve of videography as he scripted, hosted, and produced a multipart video series in the tradition of Milton and Rose Friedman's *Free to Choose*.

The series, now being finished by a professional firm, asks and answers a simple question: Why don't educational innovations that produce outstanding academic results simply sweep through our schools in the same way that, say, iPods blew away the Walkman? If the final product is anything like the rough cuts I've seen, the series will do him justice, providing a showcase not just of his research, but of the man himself.

Andrew was a generous and talented human being who worked for freedom of choice for all children in education. This is surely tribute enough, but in Andrew's case, I must add that he was a good man, and that he will be missed by virtually everyone who knew him. I join my colleagues at the Mackinac Center in wishing Andrew's family, friends, coworkers, and, most particularly, his wife, Kay Krewson, every solace in the days ahead.

Originally appeared at Mackinac.org

Darla Romfo

President, Children's Scholarship Fund

It was only after hearing about Andrew's death that I realized he must have been no more than 30 when he wrote the very compelling book, *Market Education: The Unknown History*. I knew when Ted Forstmann gave me a copy to read in 1999 that it must be an important book and that Andrew must be a very smart man since Ted, who was not one to lavish undeserved praise on anyone, insisted on how essential it was that I read *Market Education* before thinking I knew anything about education reform.

Andrew never disappointed. He was as nice as he was smart and very much a team player.

Rest in peace, Andrew. And may you find comfort, Kay, in the deep affection so many have for Andrew.

Originally appeared at ScholarhipFund.org

Doug Tuthill

President, Step Up for Students

Andrew Coulson, the gentleman-scholar at the libertarian-leaning Cato Institute, died yesterday of brain cancer. Andrew was 48.

I met Andrew in 2008, soon after I became president of Step Up for Students. I'm sure he was curious about this liberal Democrat and long-time teacher and union leader who was now leading the country's largest private school choice organization.

Andrew and I spoke and exchanged emails frequently during my first few years in this job. He was a brilliant thinker and extraordinarily polite. We shared a passion for freedom and equal opportunity, but we did occasionally disagree, and those are the discussions I cherish the most. He was sure that multiple Scholarship Funding Organizations strengthened tax credit scholarship programs, while I thought the evidence showed the contrary. We ended up agreeing to disagree.

Andrew loved facts and logic. He had an engineer's mind and was relentlessly methodical in laying out his arguments. I appreciated his commitment to civility and rationality in private and public discourse and was always influenced, if not persuaded, by his reasoning and facts.

I especially appreciated Andrew's empathy for our different roles. He would regularly end our conversations by acknowledging that it was easy to be an idealist while working at a think tank. He knew the political battles we were fighting in the Florida legislature required compromise, particularly in the area of how best to regulate choice programs.

Andrew's death is a huge loss for our movement. I will always carry our discussions with me. Hopefully I won't let him down.

Originally appeared at redefinED

Larry Sand

President, California Teachers Empowerment Network

On February 7th, Andrew Coulson tragically passed away at age 48 from brain cancer. As senior fellow in education policy at the Cato

Institute, he led the charge for free market reforms in education. An unapologetic capitalist, he believed that the market would inevitably lead to better educational outcomes for all kids. And it was really more than a belief. When the former computer engineer saw a problem, he got busy tinkering under the hood to see what the problem was and how best to fix it.

Coulson was a kind, brilliant man whose sense of humor was always at the ready. His colleagues, Jason Bedrick and Neal McCluskey, found him to be "almost impossibly sunny." Even those coming from a very different political/education angle appreciated and respected him. Reformer Doug Tuthill, a one-time union leader and self-described liberal Democrat, said of him, "Andrew loved facts and logic. He had an engineer's mind and was relentlessly methodical in laying out his arguments. I appreciated his commitment to civility and rationality in private and public discourse, and was always influenced, if not persuaded, by his reasoning and facts."

Before I met Coulson in 2010, we had a brief email relationship, and in 2009 he sent me a copy of "The Effects of Teachers Unions on American Education," a paper he wrote for the *Cato Journal*. While the teachers unions are quick to impress upon the world how much they do for teachers, they never get around to telling you specifics. Oh sure, they go on about salary and benefits, but are their claims true? Coulson, using piles of data, cut through union happy talk and left us with a very different view.

One of the claims of the teachers unions is that collective bargaining is the life-blood of the union movement, but Coulson handily debunks that. While collective bargaining has some effect on teacher salaries, it is not nearly as great as is commonly assumed.

Coulson cites Stanford economist Carolyn Hoxby, who suggests that the real union wage premium is somewhere between zero and 10 percent. Looking at rural Pennsylvania districts, economist Robert Lemke found the public school union wage premium at 7.6 percent. Cornell's Michael Lovenheim looked at three Midwestern states and concluded that "unions have no effect on teacher pay." Coulson clarifies that salary hikes have all undeniably occurred, but "they have occurred in both unionized and nonunionized public school districts."

So if salary hikes (and other collective bargaining goodies) haven't done much for union members, what have the unions accomplished for their teachers? Coulson maintained that unions protect teachers from having to compete in the educational marketplace.

Another great Coulson contribution came in the one (that I am aware of) interchange between Andrew and American Federation of Teachers president Randi Weingarten, and it didn't work out too well for the union leader. In 2011, she wrote an insufferable op-ed in the *Wall Street Journal* in which she claimed that "Markets Aren't the Education Solution." Coulson responded with "Dear Ms. Weingarten: I'll Show You Mine If You'll Show Me Yours," in which he wrote he'd "prefer to reach policy conclusions based on empirical research." As Coulson pointed out, Weingarten came to her conclusion "based on the testimony of a few foreign teachers' union leaders and government officials who . . . run official government education monopolies." Coulson produced a most interesting chart that clearly shows how many studies favor education markets over state school monopolies, and vice versa, in each of six outcome areas.

Not surprisingly, Weingarten didn't (because she couldn't) deliver a rejoinder.

Coulson nailed the subject: "The NEA [National Education Association] and AFT [American Federation of Teachers] spend large sums on political lobbying so that public school districts maintain their monopoly control of more than half a trillion dollars in annual U.S. K–12 education spending. And since both the U.S. and international research indicate that achievement and efficiency are generally higher in private sector—and particularly competitive market—education systems, the public school monopoly imposes an enormous cost on American children and taxpayers."

To further bring Coulson's thesis to light, one only needs to look at recent events. A small sampling:

In Los Angeles, the teachers union just asked for—and got—a 30 percent dues increase from its members. Its rallying cry? "We need the money to battle foes of traditional public education."

In Jefferson County, Colorado, a "parent" group led the charge to get rid of a school board majority "with an extreme anti-public education agenda." In reality, it wasn't parent-led, it was union-led. The National Education Association and its state and local affiliates fully subsidized an ugly and unfortunately successful campaign to unseat the NEA-dubbed "right-wing" school board.

In New York City, the unions are on an eternal mission to cripple Eva Moskowitz's highly successful (nonunionized) charter franchise.

Coulson's research led him to understand that we are "paying dearly for the union label, but mainly due to union lobbying to preserve the government school monopoly rather than to collective bargaining." The good news is that because of Andrew Coulson and other school choice warriors, that monopoly is unraveling, albeit very slowly. . . .

Losing Coulson was a blow for those of us who are desperately trying to minimize the damage done by the teachers unions and the government education monopoly. . . .

[His] life's work must continue; it's up to all of us to dig in and ensure that [his] efforts have not been in vain.

Originally appeared at Unionwatch.org

Jay P. Greene

Distinguished professor and head of the Department of Education Reform at the University of Arkansas

Many of you have heard the sad news that Andrew Coulson passed away over the weekend. I thought I would share some personal memories.

I first remember meeting Andrew and his wife, Kay, at a conference in Toronto in 2000. I have to admit that he felt out of place. Here was this guy without any university, think tank, or other affiliation and without any formal training presenting on the history of markets in education. And people did not typically attend these meetings with spouses. Who was this guy?

As it turns out, this guy was a brilliant autodidact who "retired" after being an early programmer with Microsoft to devote his time to studying and advocating for education reform. And he was really good at it.

The thing that struck me most about Andrew was his incredible optimism and quirky sense of humor. Liberty-oriented education activists tend to be on the losing side of policy battles. It can be downright discouraging. But Andrew never seemed discouraged or became bitter. It was a long game and he maintained a sunny optimism that freedom worked better and people would eventually gravitate toward what worked.

He didn't mind standing apart from the crowd. Just because donors, policymakers, and other scholars were drawn to test-based accountability didn't make Andrew feel like he had to join them. He even expressed serious reservations about certain methods of expanding school choice, including charters and vouchers, that he thought would invite excessive government regulation. I confess that I paid little attention to Andrew's warnings back then, but I wish I had. The experience and wisdom he obtained from studying history made him more sensitive to these dangers than my narrow practice of social science. The autodidact had quite a lot to teach highly trained people like me. As it turned out, choice reforms less prone to excessive regulation, like tax credit–funded scholarships and ESAs [education savings accounts], are now spreading rapidly—just as Andrew had expected and advised.

His humor often seemed to involve plays on words. For example, I once posted to Facebook a photo of what I (incorrectly) captioned as a "Golden Lion Tamarind." He made some sort of joke about how the dish was prepared. Some people of faith find small typos and errors in language interesting because they think they can be unintentionally prophetic. I don't know if that was Andrew's motivation, but the thought of me secretly wishing to eat a small monkey is pretty funny.

I will miss that quirky humor, but more important, I will miss his wise counsel and good cheer. It's a long game that must go on, but something will be missing without Andrew as part of it.

Originally appeared at Jay P. Greene's Blog

Michael Q. McShane

Director of education policy, Show-Me Institute

Every once in a while I stumble across a sentence and think man, I wish I'd written that. One of my favorite examples of this, and a passage that I have quoted more times than I can remember, was written by Andrew Coulson, the former director of the Cato Institute's Center for Educational Freedom, who passed away over the weekend. It came from a book he contributed to in 2002. Here's what he wrote:

> We are all losers when our differing views become declarations of war: when, instead of allowing many distinct communities of ideas to coexist harmoniously, our schools force us to battle one another in a needless and destructive fight for ideological supremacy.

Andrew's writing was the first to introduce me to the idea that school choice might not just be good for kids academically, but could help us create more harmonious communities. If we don't have to fight each other over what gets taught in history or science class, and we respect our fellow citizens' rights to instruct their children in the way that best fits their needs and their values, we can get along better with each other. What a great idea.

We truly do stand on the shoulders of giants. God bless his memory.

Originally appeared at ShowMeInstitute.org

Matthew Tabor

Editor, EducationNews.org

Andrew Coulson, senior fellow of education policy at the Cato Institute, has passed at the age of 48.

Cato colleagues Neal McCluskey and Jason Bedrick have detailed Andrew's contributions to how we think about markets in education and how we can implement what we know through systems of choice. And as Monday's podcast testifies, he took an uncommon path.

Doug Tuthill at redefinED wrote that Andrew was methodical and civil, and he influenced even those who disagreed with him. Jay Greene of the University of Arkansas's Department of Education Reform noted Andrew's humorous, witty, independent voice and his unique professional background. Nick Gillespie of Reason called him a "free market education radical"—a title carrying tremendous meaning when we consider that what seemed so radical in 1999 is reality for hundreds of thousands of kids in 2016.

Those 400,000 kids are writing their own tributes to Andrew Coulson each day without even knowing it—or him.

There are few arenas of public policy that generate cults of personality quite the way education does. Tribalism and the desire to deify (or demonize) people associated with a particular ideology are forces so strong that throwing out a name or two has become shorthand for laying bare one's entire educational belief system. The movers and shakers in education jockey for position in that ecosystem, growing their brand and habitually checking their rankings (Whose rankings? Anyone who will rank them, and for anything) as they compel their supporters to wage battles via proxy on social media and in school board meetings.

They sell, sell, sell. It doesn't get us anywhere, and it's uncomfortable. Great for the individual, not so great for the problem they're trying to solve.

But a few people just plain work. They offer something new, explain why it's better than what we've got, and make a case compelling enough to fuel a movement. They shore up that case obsessively and make adjustments as evidence dictates. They understand the most important concept in sales: people hate to be sold to, but they love to buy. They focus on creating intellectual products people want to buy, and they have one overarching goal: moving the needle.

Andrew Coulson moved the needle.

Over a decade ago when I was transitioning into education policy, someone suggested that I read *Market Education: The Unknown History*. I won't go over the contents of the book—you've either already read it, or you're about to—but I was struck by how much Coulson knew. This guy has a command of virtually every topic under the sun, and what kind of background allowed for that? A little Googling showed that, on paper, he had no business writing that book. Yet there it was, and it was remarkable.

I found the PhD program I was in to be a useless grind, so I talked with a professor/friend about how you can do something like this—I had *Market Education* in my bag, so I held it out—without trudging through tired, narrow academic channels. He said, "Well, really. . .you can't."

I said, "You can." I had a book to wave in the air that proved it. He just had words and a slavish devotion to academia, so I chalked it up as a win.

I skipped out on the PhD program after receiving an email that asked grad students to classify the ethnicities of student research subjects by their surnames for part of an education-related study. The pay was $20/hour, but I wouldn't have done that for $2,000/hour. I had proof that I could advance my studies elsewhere, ethically, in a broad range of fields, and come out all right—so I spent the next 10 years working on a hundred different topics in a dozen different places. I was right and my academic friend was wrong.

Years later, I crossed paths with Andrew Coulson himself through mutual friends on Facebook. He proved himself to be a "gentleman-scholar," as Doug Tuthill wrote. I never met him in person, but if I had, I would have called him Mr. Coulson.

I saw credentialism dominate many different fields in many different countries, enough so that I stopped caring where anyone went to school or what letters they had before or after their names. Titles indicated how or where someone spent a block of time, and anything beyond that was a crap shoot. I hate credentialism.

Over the last year or so, I had friendly exchanges with Mr. Coulson—and I followed along closely with the discussions I wasn't a part of.

They were master classes in wit, analysis, and advocacy. That I had access to them at a cost of nothing more than my time was an almost-daily lottery win. I half-stalked the poor guy professionally, but I wasn't about to waste the opportunity.

Through those back-and-forths about every facet of school choice and its related disciplines, I gained an incredible amount of knowledge from Mr. Coulson—and he exposed himself to be a good man. You can't go to school for that. You don't apply, pay tuition, or take up space in a classroom, and there's no certificate at the end. It takes more time, more work, and comes at a greater cost. It's a lot harder to do.

A good man deserves a title that reflects the respect he's earned rather than a title he has forced the world to acknowledge because of some series of endeavors that the world may or may not find value in. A good man is a Mister. It's the highest title anyone can hold.

I am, for the most part, tied to a desk and manning its requisite nerd-box. That is by choice. Mr. Coulson was limited lately by circumstance, but we both seemed to have had the blessings of a few windows and a little bit of time outside. I posted a photo of Grommit, the little rabbit with an off-center tail who marshaled our Cooperstown, New York, lawn with an uncommon competence. Mr. Coulson regaled me with the occasional update about Pamplemousse, the critter who does whatever it is that critters do on lawns in the Pacific Northwest.

That's the hard part about not taking that narrow, well-defined path—there aren't too many people who you know are doing something like you're doing each day, then stopping to look out a window to anthropomorphize bunnies. When you come across someone who you recognize might spend 15 seconds of his day the same way you do, it matters. When you come across someone like that who also takes you seriously, it really matters.

I regret that Mr. Coulson didn't know anything I've written here. I never told him or anyone else. And I regret that I won't have the opportunity to change his mind on the only two issues of substance that we disagreed on—the importance of sports in culture (I am a fan, he seemed disinterested) and verb agreement with collective nouns (I insist collective nouns are singular, while he said the British plural approach was supreme). Given another 60 or so years of debate, I do believe I could have converted him on both scores—because I, like Mr. Coulson, am something of a Sisyphean optimist with those things.

Andrew Coulson has passed, leaving behind an impressive body of work and a legacy that's a little part of the life force of hundreds of thousands of kids, their families, and their communities. Those numbers are poised to multiply.

I still don't know what, if any, official credentials he had. Someone might tell me, but I won't bother to look them up. I don't need to. I know that he advanced the work of countless others, including mine, and helped lead a successful movement that decades ago seemed impossible. He did it with humility, civility, and a seriousness of purpose.

There are 1,300 words above, but five probably would've sufficed: Mr. Coulson moved the needle.

Originally appeared at EducationNews.org

Joshua P. Thompson

Senior attorney, Pacific Legal Foundation

Liberty lost one of her staunchest defenders yesterday morning, when Andrew Coulson passed away after a 15-month battle with brain cancer. Andrew was a senior fellow in education policy at the Cato Institute. In that position, Andrew researched, published, and advocated for school choice.

I have long been an admirer of Andrew Coulson's work—even before I began my career at Pacific Legal Foundation. His book, *Market Education,* has long been a staple on my bookshelf. Andrew and I first crossed paths professionally when I posted a critique of an op-ed he wrote in the *Philadelphia Inquirer*. His response led to a very interesting back and forth. . . . Despite our minor disagreement, that conversation led us to more closely follow the other's work. We'd exchange emails now and then, usually when one of us had something interesting to say about school choice. For National School Choice Week last year, Andrew Coulson appeared with me on a PLF [Pacific Legal Foundation] podcast. The podcast remains one of our most popular ever. Andrew and I discussed a lot of the contemporary issues facing advocates of educational freedom today.

It was during the preparation for that podcast last year that I first learned about Andrew's diagnosis. He was undergoing treatment at the time and had to schedule the taping around his doctor visits. I, of course, volunteered to postpone the podcast to a more convenient time, but Andrew insisted. He wasn't going to let his treatment get in the way of advocating for freedom.

Rest in peace, Andrew Coulson. "Thankfully, his ideas remain, and they will always illuminate the pathway forward."

Originally appeared at Pacific Legal Foundation Liberty Blog

About the Contributors

Bob Bowdon is the founder of Choice Media and the Choice Media smartphone app for education news. He has been a television producer, reporter, and commentator for PBS, Bloomberg Television, and national syndication. He also appeared as a recurring character in satirical news sketches for the Onion News Network. *The Cartel*, Bowdon's documentary, reveals the nature and extent of corruption in public education. The film won a dozen film festival awards, Warner Brothers distribution, and a national theatrical release.

George A. Clowes is a Heartland Institute senior fellow addressing education policy. He served as founding managing editor of *School Reform News* between November 1996 and January 2005. In 2001, he helped develop The *Heartland [School Reform] Plan for Illinois*, and in 2008, he authored a research study on lessons from the Milwaukee voucher program, called *Can Vouchers Reform Public Schools?* Born and raised in England, he received a doctorate degree from the University of Manchester Institute of Science and Technology in 1965 and was a Fulbright Scholar conducting research in biochemistry at Northwestern University from 1965 to 1967. Clowes spent most of his career in the private sector, working at various times as a research chemist, software developer/database manager, and market research director. He also ran for public office in the Village of Mount Prospect, serving one term as park district commissioner and two terms as village trustee.

Jay P. Greene is a distinguished professor and head of the Department of Education Reform at the University of Arkansas. Greene's current areas of research interest include school choice, culturally enriching field trips, and the effect of schools on noncognitive and civic values. He is also known for his work on improving the accurate reporting of high school graduation rates, addressing financial incentives in special education, and the use of standardized tests to curb social promotion. His research was cited four times in the Supreme Court's opinions in the landmark *Zelman v. Simmons-Harris* case on school vouchers.

His articles have appeared in several academic journals, including *Education Finance and Policy*, *Economics of Education Review*, *Educational Evaluation and Policy Analysis*, *Educational Researcher*, and *Sociology of Education*. Greene has been a professor of government at the University of Texas at Austin and the University of Houston. He received his BA in history from Tufts University in 1988 and his PhD in government from Harvard University in 1995.

John Merrifield is a professor of economics at the University of Texas at San Antonio, a position he has held since 1987. He is the author of four books, including *The School Choice Wars*, *School Choices*, and *Parental Choice as an Education Reform Catalyst: Global Lessons*. Merrifield is the former editor of the *Journal of School Choice* and currently is the editor of the *School System Reform Journal*. He has also written 45 articles published in peer-reviewed journals and several book chapters in his primary teaching and research fields of education economics, urban and regional economics, environmental and natural resource economics, and public finance. Merrifield received a BS in natural resource management from Cal Poly San Luis Obispo in 1977, an MA in economic geography from the University of Illinois in 1979, and a PhD in economics from the University of Wyoming in 1984.

Adam B. Schaeffer is the founder of Evolving Strategies, a clinical data science firm, and a former policy analyst at Cato's Center for Educational Freedom. He's consumed by an itch to understand what makes people tick and why they think and do the things they do. To that end, his firm uses randomized-controlled message trials and artificial intelligence to modify (not just predict) human behavior. Schaeffer received his PhD from the University of Virginia in political psychology and behavior. His dissertation assessed how different combinations of school choice policies and messages can expand and mobilize elite and mass support. He received his MA in social science from the University of Chicago, where his thesis integrated aspects of evolutionary theory and psychology with political theory and strategy. His academic research and teaching centered on social psychology and human behavior, and that emphasis continues to animate his applied research. He considers himself akin to a research biologist who has the great privilege of studying the behavior of the most complex and fascinating animal on the planet: Homo sapiens.

James Tooley is a professor of education policy at Newcastle University. There he is the director of the E. G. West Centre, which is dedicated to choice, competition, and entrepreneurship in education. He has done extensive work in demonstrating the benefits of private education for low-income families. Much of his work has focused on identifying ways to make private education more accessible and to facilitate its growth in the developing world, especially among the poor. Tooley has worked for over 25 years in educational development, including years of on-location experience in Ghana, Nigeria, India, and Honduras. He has served as a researcher at Manchester and Oxford universities. His books include *The Beautiful Tree: A Personal Journey into How the World's Poorest People Are Educating Themselves* (2009), *Imprisoned in India: Corruption and Extortion in the World's Largest Democracy* (2016), *From Village School to Global Brand: Changing the World through Education* (2012), and *Reclaiming Education* (2000).

About the Editors

Jason Bedrick is director of policy with EdChoice and a former policy analyst with the Cato Institute's Center for Educational Freedom. He also served as a legislator in the New Hampshire House of Representatives and was an education policy research fellow at the Josiah Bartlett Center for Public Policy. Bedrick has published numerous studies on educational choice programs with organizations such as EdChoice, the Heritage Foundation, the Texas Public Policy Foundation, the Pioneer Institute, the Show-Me Institute, and the Caesar Rodney Institute. His articles have been featured in the *New York Post, Boston Globe, Palm Beach Post, Fort Worth Star-Telegram, Las Vegas Review-Journal, New Hampshire Union Leader, National Review, National Affairs, Education Next, Federalist,* and *Townhall.com*. Bedrick received his master's degree in public policy from the John F. Kennedy School of Government at Harvard University, where he was a fellow at the Taubman Center for State and Local Government. His thesis, "Choosing to Learn," assessed scholarship tax credit programs operating in eight states, including their program design, impact on student performance, fiscal impact, and popularity.

Neal P. McCluskey is the director of the Cato Institute's Center for Educational Freedom. Prior to arriving at Cato, McCluskey served in the U.S. Army, taught high-school English, and was a freelance reporter covering municipal government and education in suburban New Jersey. More recently, he was a policy analyst at the Center for Education Reform. McCluskey is the author of the book *Feds in the Classroom: How Big Government Corrupts, Cripples, and Compromises American Education*, and his writings have appeared in such publications as the *Wall Street Journal, Washington Post*, and *Forbes*. In addition to his written work, McCluskey has appeared on C-SPAN, CNN, the Fox News Channel, and numerous radio programs. McCluskey holds an undergraduate degree from Georgetown University, where he double-majored in government and English, a master's degree in political science from Rutgers University, and a PhD in public policy from George Mason University.

Notes

Chapter 2

1. Andrew J. Coulson, "Forging Consensus: Can the School Choice Community Come Together on an Explicit Goal and a Plan for Achieving It?" Mackinac Center for Public Policy, April 2004.

2. Andrew J. Coulson, *Market Education: The Unknown History* (New Brunswick, NJ: Social Philosophy and Policy Center and Transaction Publishers, 1999).

3. See Jason Bedrick, Jonathan Butcher, and Clint Bolick, "Taking Credit for Education: How to Fund Education Savings Accounts through Tax Credits," Cato Institute Policy Analysis no. 785, January 20, 2016.

4. Coulson, "Forging Consensus," p. 11.

5. Coulson, "Forging Consensus," p. 11.

6. For an extensive discussion of the legal issues in each state, with relevant case law, see Richard D. Komer and Olivia Grady, "School Choice and State Constitutions: A Guide to Designing School Choice Programs," 2nd ed., The Institute for Justice and The American Legislative Exchange Council, September 2016.

7. *Arizona Christian School Tuition Organization v. Winn*, 563 U.S. 125 (2011) 14, http://ij.org/wp-content/uploads/2000/02/usss_winn_decision.pdf.

8. *Colorado Congress of Parents, Teachers and Students v. Owens*, 03SA364 (Col. 2004); *Holmes v. Bush*, 04-2323 (Fla. 2006); *Jackson v. Benson*, 97-0270 (Wis. 1998); *Simmons-Harris v. Goff*, 97-1117 (Ohio 1999). The courts in *Jackson v. Benson* and *Simmons-Harris v. Goff* did not dispute that the voucher funds were public funds but ruled that they did not violate the constitutional provisions under consideration because the parents rather than the state were the recipients of those funds.

9. *Holmes v. Bush*, 04-2323 (Fla. 2006). The Florida Supreme Court ruling has been rightly criticized as an exercise in unalloyed political activism from the bench, and it demonstrates that some courts will find little restraint in the letter and intent of state constitutional provisions. Tax credits are therefore not exempt from such misuses of judicial authority. The ruling under consideration here, however, relied on the status of vouchers as "public funds" in overturning the Florida Opportunity Scholarship program. To overturn tax credits, the court would need to find, contrary to widespread legal precedent, that they are "public funds" or develop an even more novel objection.

The following excerpts have italics added for emphasis. The summary of the ruling stated: "The issue we decide is whether the State of Florida is prohibited by the Florida Constitution from *expending public funds* to allow students to obtain an independent school education in kindergarten through grade twelve, as an alternative to a public school education." The court ruled that the program is a violation of the uniformity provision because "it diverts *public dollars* into separate private systems parallel to and in competition with the free public schools that are the sole means set out in the Constitution for the state to provide for the education of Florida's children. This diversion not only reduces money available to the free schools, but also funds independent schools that are not 'uniform' when compared with each other or the public system. Many standards imposed by law on the public schools are inapplicable to the independent schools receiving *public monies*." The legal distinction between public and private funds is central to this ruling overturning vouchers just as it has been central in rulings upholding tax credits in other states.

10. Laura Langer and Paul Brace, "The Preemptive Power of State Supreme Courts: Adoption of Abortion and Death Penalty Legislation," *Policy Studies Journal* 33 (2005): 317–40.

11. Langer and Brace, "The Preemptive Power of State Supreme Courts," 331.

12. See, for example, Jason Bedrick, "Nevada Supreme Court: Education Savings Accounts Are Constitutional, Funding Mechanism Isn't," *Cato at Liberty*, September 29, 2016, https://www.cato.org/blog/nevada-supreme-court-education-savings-accounts-are-constitutional-funding-mechanism-isnt.

13. Andrew D. Catt, "Public Rules on Private Schools: Measuring the Regulatory Impact of State Statutes and School Choice Programs," Friedman Foundation for Educational Choice, May 2014.

14. U.S. Department of Agriculture, "Supplemental Nutrition Assistance Program (SNAP): Eligible Food Items," March 21, 2016, https://www.fns.usda.gov/snap/eligible-food-items.

15. See Tracy Moore, "Drug Tests for Food Stamps: Terrible Policy, by the Numbers," *Vocativ*, April 14, 2016.

16. Paul E. Peterson, Michael B. Henderson, Martin R. West, and Samuel Barrows, "Results from the 2016 *Education Next Poll*," *Education Next*, http://educationnext.org/2016-ednext-poll-interactive/.

17. See iPOLL databases of opinion polling for multiple polls on tax credit policies, https://ropercenter.cornell.edu/CFIDE/cf/action/home/index.cfm.

18. Andrew LeFevre, personal communication, August 9, 2007.

19. For information regarding the pervasive problems for collective action in politics, see Mancur Olson, *The Logic of Collective Action: Public Goods and the Theory of Groups* (Cambridge, MA: Harvard University Press, 1971); Sidney Tarrow, *Power in Movement: Social Movements, Collective Action and Politics* (Cambridge, MA: Cambridge University Press, 1998); and Kristin A. Goss, *The Missing Movement for Gun Control in America* (Princeton, NJ: Princeton University Press, 2006).

20. Florida House of Representatives, CS/HB 1009, Florida Tax Credit Scholarship Program, http://www.myfloridahouse.gov/Sections/Bills/billsdetail.aspx?BillId=43675.

Chapter 3

1. Andrew J. Coulson, "Forging Consensus: Can the School Choice Community Come Together on an Explicit Goal and a Plan for Achieving It?" Mackinac Center for Public Policy, April 2004.

2. George A. Clowes, "Still No Consensus on School Choice," The Heartland Institute, April 1, 2004. See also Andrew J. Coulson, "Forging Consensus: Comments by George Clowes and Jay P. Greene, with Responses from the Author," Mackinac Center for Public Policy, September 1, 2005.

3. Andrew J. Coulson, "On the Way to School: Why and How to Make a Market in Education," Cato Institute, p. 4. An edited version appeared in *Freedom and School Choice in American Education*, ed. Greg Forster and C. Bradley Thompson (New York: Palgrave Macmillan, June 2011).

4. George A. Clowes, "The Design of School Choice Programs: A Systems Approach," *Freedom and School Choice in American Education*, ed. Greg Forster and C. Bradley Thompson (New York: Palgrave Macmillan, June 2011).

5. Andrew J. Coulson, "Toward Market Education: Are Vouchers or Tax Credits the Better Path?" Cato Institute Policy Analysis no. 392, February 22, 2001.

6. Andrew J. Coulson, *Market Education: The Unknown History* (New Brunswick, NJ: Social Philosophy and Policy Center and Transaction Publishers, 1999).

7. Coulson, *Market Education*.

8. Coulson, "Forging Consensus."

9. Clowes, "The Design of School Choice Programs."

10. Milton Friedman, "The Role of Government in Education," in *Economics and the Public Interest*, ed. Robert A. Solo (New Brunswick, NJ: Rutgers University Press, 1955).

11. Albert Shanker, "Put Merit in Merit Schools," American Federation of Teachers "Where We Stand" column, *New York Times*, July 23, 1989.

12. Shanker, "Put Merit in Merit Schools."

13. Milton Friedman, "School Vouchers Turn 50," *School Choice Advocate*, November 2005.

14. John Merrifield, "Dismal Science: The Shortcomings of U.S. School Choice Research and How to Address Them," Cato Institute Policy Analysis no. 616, April 16, 2008.

15. George A. Clowes, "With the Right Design, Vouchers Can Reform Public Schools: Lessons from the Milwaukee Parental Choice Program," *Journal of School Choice* 2, no. 4 (2008): 367–91.

16. Paul E. Peterson, "The Theory and Practice of School Choice," Federal Reserve Bank of Dallas conference proceedings, October 2003. See also Marguerite Roza and Jon Fullerton, "School Funding Practices Keep Dollars in Districts for 'Phantom Students,'" *Education Next*, May 1, 2013.

17. In the original study, only "imminent" and "specific" were identified, but "well-publicized" fits the facts and its use seems appropriate in better defining what is meant by "explicit" competition.

18. National Alliance for Public Charter Schools website, "2015 Annual Report," May 16, 2016.

19. Lisa Snell, "Defining the Education Market: Reconsidering Charter Schools," *Cato Journal* 25, no. 2 (Spring/Summer 2005): 267–77. See also George A. Clowes, "What Does It Take to Create a Marketplace in Education?" *School Reform News*, December 1, 2004.

20. The Center for Education Reform website, "All about Charter Schools: Quick Facts," July 22, 2016.

21. National Alliance for Public Charter Schools website, "Facts about Charters: Are Charter Schools For-Profit?"

22. Katie Ash, "For-Profit Charter Management Organizations Expand Reach, Report Says," *Education Week*, December 4, 2013.

23. KIPP Foundation, website "KIPP Schools."

24. Ted Rebarber and Alison Consoletti Zgainer, eds., "Survey of America's Charter Schools 2014," Center for Education Reform, 2014.

25. EdChoice website, "School Choice: Florida Tax Credit Scholarship Program."

26. Florida Department of Education website, "Student Enrollment (FTE) History: 2015-16 Final FTE."

27. Private School Review website, "Florida Private Schools."

28. EdChoice, *The ABCs of School Choice: 2015 Edition* (Indianapolis, IN: Friedman Foundation for Educational Choice, 2015).

29. Florida Department of Education, "Annual Financial Report: Expenditures per Unweighted Full-Time Equivalent (UFTE), FY 2014–15."

30. Florida Department of Education, "Student Enrollment (FTE) History: FY 2014–15."

31. Florida Department of Education, "Florida Tax Credit Scholarship Program: February 2016 Quarterly Report," February 2016

32. Hispanic Council for Reform and Educational Options (HCREO), "Grading Arizona's Scholarship Organizations," August 2014.

33. EdChoice website, "School Choice: Arizona—Original Individual Income Tax Credit Scholarship Program."

34. Diane M. Douglas, "Fall Enrollment Data," *Annual Report of the Arizona Superintendent of Public Instruction: Volume I: Fiscal Year 2014–2015* (Phoenix, AZ: Arizona Department of Education, January 16, 2016), p. 9.

35. Diane M. Douglas, "Percent of Revenue by Year by Source: Total Revenues," *Annual Report of the Arizona Superintendent of Public Instruction: Volume I: Fiscal Year 2014–2015* (Phoenix, AZ: Arizona Department of Education, January 16, 2016), p. 6.

36. EdChoice website, "School Choice: Arizona—Low-Income Corporate Income Tax Credit Scholarship Program."

37. Abraham M. Lackman, "The Collapse of Catholic School Enrollment: The Unintended Consequence of the Charter School Movement," *Albany Government Law Review* 6 (2012): 1–20.

38. Richard Buddin, "The Impact of Charter Schools on Public and Private School Enrollments," Cato Institute Policy Analysis no. 707, August 28, 2012.

39. National Education Association, "Rankings of the States 2015 and Estimates of School Statistics 2016," NEA Research, May 2016.

40. Coulson, "Toward Market Education."

41. EdChoice, *The ABCs of School Choice: 2016 Edition* (Indianapolis, IN: Friedman Foundation for Educational Choice, 2016).

42. Joseph L. Bast, "The Heartland Plan for Illinois: Model School Voucher Legislation," Heartland Institute Policy Study no. 98, May 1, 2002.

43. Herbert J. Walberg and Joseph L. Bast, *Education and Capitalism* (Stanford, CA: Hoover Institution Press, 2004), p. 301.

44. Coulson, "Forging Consensus."

45. Jason Bedrick and Lindsey M. Burke, "On Designing K–12 Education Savings Accounts," *Education Next*, January 26, 2015.

46. Coulson, "Toward Market Education."

47. Coulson, "Forging Consensus."

48. George A. Clowes, "Cleveland Parents Don't Choose Voucher Schools, Say Opponents," *School Reform News*, May 1, 2002.

49. Justice Clarence Thomas, *Mitchell v. Helms*, 530 U.S. 793 (2000).

50. Richard D. Komer, "School Choice and State Constitutions' Religion Clauses," *Journal of School Choice* 3, no. 4 (2009): 331–52.

51. Coulson, "Toward Market Education."

52. Andrew J. Coulson, "Do Vouchers and Tax Credits Increase Private School Regulation?" Cato Institute Working Paper no. 1, October 5, 2010.

53. Andrew D. Catt, "Public Rules on Private Schools: Measuring the Regulatory Impact of State Statutes and School Choice Programs," Friedman Foundation for Educational Choice, May 2014.

54. David Stuit and Sy Doan, "School Choice Regulations: Red Tape or Red Herring?" Thomas B. Fordham Institute, January 2013.

55. Brian Kisida, Patrick J. Wolf, and Evan Rhinesmith, "Views from Private Schools: Attitudes about School Choice Programs in Three States," American Enterprise Institute, January 2015.

56. Stuit and Doan, "School Choice Regulations."

57. Stuit and Doan, "School Choice Regulations," p. 31.

58. Joseph L. Bast, "Fiscal Impact of Proposed Tuition Tax Credits for the State of New Jersey," Heartland Institute Policy Study no. 96, April 2001.

59. George A. Clowes, "Tax Credits Would Boost Private Schooling in New Jersey," *School Reform News*, June 2001.

60. Clowes, "Tax Credits Would Boost Private Schooling in New Jersey."

61. David N. Figlio and Cassandra M. D. Hart, "Competitive Effects of Means-Tested School Vouchers," National Bureau of Economic Research Working Paper no. 16056, June 2010.

62. Adam B. Schaeffer, "The Public Education Tax Credit," Cato Institute Policy Analysis no. 605, December 5, 2007.

63. Coulson, "Forging Consensus."

64. Clowes, "The Design of School Choice Programs."

65. Clowes, "The Design of School Choice Programs."

66. An education savings account was added to the original proposal, which was developed before the creation of ESAs based on Milton Friedman's "partial vouchers."

67. A property tax rebate was originally specified for this option, which is based on a 1988 Heartland Institute proposal, but Coulson's argument regarding the benefits of tax credits not being public money convinced me to convert this provision to a tax credit.

68. Jay P. Greene, "The Union War on Charter Schools," *Wall Street Journal*, April 16, 2009.

Chapter 4

1. EdChoice, *The ABCs of School Choice: 2016 Edition* (Indianapolis, IN: Friedman Foundation for Educational Choice, 2016).

2. See, for example, Andrew J. Coulson, "Giving Credit Where It's Due," *The Independent Review* 7, no. 2 (Fall 2002): 278. "Although I recommend the adoption of tax credits over vouchers wherever possible, I do not oppose the passage of voucher legislation in states that knowingly choose that course."

3. Andrew J. Coulson, *Market Education: The Unknown History* (New Brunswick, NJ: Social Philosophy and Policy Center and Transaction Publishers, 1999), p. 293.

4. Andrew J. Coulson, "Comparing Public, Private, and Market Schools: The International Evidence," *Journal of School Choice* 3 (2009): 31–54.

5. Andrew J. Coulson, "On the Way to School: Why and How to Make a Market in Education," Cato Institute, p. 4. An edited version appeared in *Freedom and School Choice in American Education*, ed. Greg Forster and C. Bradley Thompson (New York: Palgrave Macmillan, June 2011).

6. Coulson, "On the Way to School," p. 2.

7. Coulson, "Giving Credit Where It's Due," p. 278.

8. See, for example, Andrew J. Coulson, "A 'Winn' for Education and Freedom of Conscience," *Huffington Post*, April 12, 2011.

9. Jason Bedrick, Jonathan Butcher, and Clint Bolick, "Taking Credit for Education: How to Fund Education Savings Accounts through Tax Credits," Cato Institute Policy Analysis no. 785, January 20, 2016.

10. *Zelman v. Simmons-Harris*, 536 U.S. 639 (2002).

11. Coulson, "Giving Credit Where It's Due," p. 281.

12. Although technically a tax credit program, Alabama's credits are "refundable," meaning that a taxpayer who does not have a large enough tax liability to take full advantage of the credit would receive the difference in the form of a "rebate" from the

state treasury. Unlike true tax credits, so-called "refundable" credits are indistinguishable from vouchers, and the Alabama Supreme Court's ruling would apply equally to a traditional voucher program.

13. Richard D. Komer and Olivia Grady, "School Choice and State Constitutions: A Guide to Designing School Choice Programs, Second Edition," Institute for Justice and The American Legislative Exchange Council, September 2016. The states in which the Institute for Justice believes the state supreme court's jurisprudence in interpreting their compelled support clause and/or Blaine Amendment would prohibit publicly funding school choice include Alaska, California, Delaware, Hawaii, Idaho, Kentucky, Massachusetts, Michigan, Missouri, New Hampshire, New Mexico, Oregon, South Dakota, Vermont, Virginia, Washington, and Wyoming.

14. One exception is Michigan, where the state constitution explicitly forbids both public funding and tax credits for all private education (not just religious schools).

15. Coulson, "A 'Winn' for Education."

16. Again, with the exception of Michigan. See note 14.

17. Coulson, "On the Way to School," p. 11.

18. Coulson, "On the Way to School," p. 15.

19. Matt Frendewey et al., "Teach Choice: 2015–2016 School Choice Yearbook," American Federation for Children Growth Fund, 2016, p. 11.

20. EdChoice website, "School Choice: Indiana—School Scholarship Tax Credit."

21. EdChoice website, "School Choice: Indiana—Choice Scholarship Program."

22. Although the voucher program was enacted in 2008, it was only expanded statewide in 2012. For enrollment figures, see EdChoice website, "School Choice: Louisiana."

23. Andrew J. Coulson, "Do Vouchers and Tax Credits Increase Private School Regulation? A Statistical Analysis," *Journal of School Choice* 5 (2011):1–29.

24. Andrew D. Catt, "Public Rules on Private Schools: Measuring the Regulatory Impact of State Statutes and School Choice Programs," Friedman Foundation for Educational Choice, May 2014, p. 4.

25. See, for example, Tracey Weinstein of the group Students First, "Does Nevada's New ESA Law Hold Promise for Kids?" Fordham Institute, June 16, 2015.

Chapter 5

1. Andrew J. Coulson, "On the Way to School: Why and How to Make a Market in Education," Cato Institute, p. 2. An edited version appeared in *Freedom and School Choice in American Education*, ed. Greg Forster and C. Bradley Thompson (New York: Palgrave Macmillan, June 2011).

2. Andrew J. Coulson, *Market Education: The Unknown History* (New Brunswick, NJ: Social Philosophy and Policy Center and Transaction Publishers, 1999), pp. 73–74.

3. Coulson, *Market Education*, p. 84.

4. Coulson, *Market Education*, p. 93.

5. Coulson, *Market Education*, pp. 93–94. See also James Tooley, *E. G. West: Economic Liberalism and the Role of Government in Education* (London: Bloomsbury Academic Press, 2008), p. 81. "Concerning widespread literacy, a report from 1838, for instance, showed that 87 percent of *pauper* children aged 9 to 16 years old housed in the workhouses of Norfolk and Suffolk could read to some extent."

6. Coulson, *Market Education*, p. 94.

7. Jason Bedrick, "The Folly of Overregulating School Choice," *Education Next*, January 5, 2016.

8. Coulson, *Market Education*, p. 85.
9. Coulson, *Market Education*, p. 85.
10. Coulson, *Market Education*, pp. 82–83.

Chapter 6

1. James Tooley, *The Beautiful Tree: A Personal Journey into How the World's Poorest People Are Educating Themselves* (Washington: Cato Institute, 2009).
2. Andrew J. Coulson, "An 'Invisible Hand' Up," *Philanthropy*, July/August 2007.
3. Andrew J. Coulson, *Market Education: The Unknown History* (New Brunswick, NJ: Social Philosophy and Policy Center and Transaction Publishers, 1999).
4. Andrew J. Coulson, "Education and Indoctrination in the Muslim World: Is There a Problem? What Can We Do about It?" Cato Institute Policy Analysis no. 511, March 11, 2004, p. 20.
5. Lant Pritchett, *The Rebirth of Education: Schooling Ain't Learning* (Washington: Center for Global Development, 2013), p. 171.
6. Coulson, "Education and Indoctrination in the Muslim World?" p. 15.
7. Coulson, "Education and Indoctrination in the Muslim World?" p. 17.
8. Coulson, "Education and Indoctrination in the Muslim World?" p. 17.
9. Coulson, "Education and Indoctrination in the Muslim World?" p. 17.
10. Coulson, "Education and Indoctrination in the Muslim World?" p. 17.
11. Coulson, "Education and Indoctrination in the Muslim World?" p. 18.
12. Coulson, "Education and Indoctrination in the Muslim World?" p. 18.
13. Coulson, "Education and Indoctrination in the Muslim World?" p. 18.
14. Coulson, "Education and Indoctrination in the Muslim World?" p. 20.
15. Coulson, "Education and Indoctrination in the Muslim World?" p. 24.
16. James Tooley, "Big Questions and Poor Economics: Banerjee and Duflo on Schooling in Developing Countries," *Econ Journal Watch* 9, no. 3 (2012): 170–85.
17. Coulson, "Education and Indoctrination in the Muslim World?" p. 24.
18. Andrew J. Coulson, "Comparing Public, Private, and Market Schools: The International Evidence," *Journal of School Choice* 3, no. 1 (2009): 31–54.
19. Andrew J. Coulson, "Market Education and Its Critics: Testing School Choice Criticisms against the International Evidence," in *What America Can Learn from School Choice in Other Countries*, ed. David Salisbury and James Tooley (Washington: Cato Institute, 2005).
20. Coulson, "Comparing Public, Private, and Market Schools," p. 31.
21. Coulson, "Comparing Public, Private, and Market Schools," p. 32.
22. Coulson, "Comparing Public, Private, and Market Schools," p. 33.
23. Coulson, "Comparing Public, Private, and Market Schools," p. 33.
24. Coulson, "Comparing Public, Private, and Market Schools," p. 33.
25. Coulson, "Comparing Public, Private, and Market Schools," p. 35.
26. Coulson, "Comparing Public, Private, and Market Schools," p. 31.
27. Coulson, "Comparing Public, Private, and Market Schools," p. 40.
28. Coulson, "Comparing Public, Private, and Market Schools," p. 41.
29. Coulson, "Comparing Public, Private, and Market Schools," p. 41.
30. Coulson, "Comparing Public, Private, and Market Schools," p. 47.
31. Coulson, "Comparing Public, Private, and Market Schools," p. 47.
32. Coulson, "Comparing Public, Private, and Market Schools," p. 47.
33. Coulson, "Comparing Public, Private, and Market Schools," p. 47.

34. Coulson, "Comparing Public, Private, and Market Schools," p. 47.

35. Tooley, *Beautiful Tree;* James Tooley et al., "The Relative Quality and Cost-Effectiveness of Private and Public Schools for Low-Income Families: A Case Study in a Developing Country," *School Effectiveness and School Improvement* 21, no. 2 (2010): 117–44; James Tooley et al., "School Choice and Academic Performance: Some Evidence from Developing Countries," *Journal of School Choice* 5, no. 1 (2011): 1–39; and Pauline Dixon, James Tooley, and Ian Schagen, "The Relative Quality of Private and Public Schools for Low-Income Families Living in Slums of Nairobi, Kenya," in *Low-Fee Private Schooling: Aggravating Equity or Mitigating Disadvantage?* ed. Prachi Srivastava (Oxford, UK: Symposium Books, 2013).

36. James Tooley and David Longfield, "Private Education in Low-Income Areas of Monrovia: School and Household Surveys," working paper, E. G. West Centre, Newcastle University, United Kingdom, and Development Initiatives Liberia Inc., November 2013, https://egwestcentre.com/publications-3/working-papers/.

37. James Tooley and David Longfield, "Private Primary Education in Western Area, Sierra Leone," working paper, E. G. West Centre, Newcastle University, United Kingdom, and People's Educational Association, September 2013.

38. David Longfield and James Tooley, "A Survey of Schools in Juba," working paper, E. G. West Centre, Newcastle University, United Kingdom, and Nile Institute, November 2013.

39. James Tooley and David Longfield, "Affordability of Private Schools: Exploration of a Conundrum and Towards a Definition of 'Low-Cost,'" *Oxford Review of Education* 42, no. 4 (2016): 444–59.

40. James Tooley and Pauline Dixon, "'*De Facto*' Privatisation of Education and the Poor: Implications of a Study from Sub-Saharan Africa and India," *Compare* 36, no. 4 (2006): 443–62; and Caine Rolleston and Modupe Adefeso-Olateju, "De Facto Privatisation of Basic Education in Africa: A Market Response to Government Failure? A Comparative Study of the Cases of Ghana and Nigeria," in *Education, Privatisation and Social Justice: Case Studies from Africa, South Asia and South East Asia,* ed. Ian Macpherson, Susan Robertson, and Geoffrey Walford (Oxford, UK: Symposium Books, 2014).

41. James Tooley, "Extending Access to Low-Cost Private Schools through Vouchers: An Alternative Interpretation of a Two-Stage 'School Choice' Experiment in India," *Oxford Review of Education* 42, no. 5 (2016): 579–93; and Karthik Muralidharan and Venkatesh Sundararaman, "The Aggregate Effect of School Choice: Evidence from a Two-Stage Experiment in India," *Quarterly Journal of Economics* 130, no. 3 (2015): 1011–66.

42. Tooley, "Extending Access to Low-Cost Private Schools through Vouchers."

Chapter 7

1. Many of these ideas are laid out in Adam B. Schaeffer, "The Public Education Tax Credit," Cato Institute Policy Analysis no. 605, December 5, 2007.

2. Andrew J. Coulson, *Market Education: The Unknown History* (New Brunswick, NJ: Social Philosophy and Policy Center and Transaction Publishers, 1999).

3. John Merrifield, *The School Choice Wars* (Lanham, MD: Scarecrow Press, 2001); and John Merrifield and Nathan Gray, "An Evaluation of the CEO Horizon, 1998–2008, Edgewood Tuition Voucher Program," working paper, August 31, 2009.

4. John Merrifield, "Education Freedom Index," School System Reform Studies website.

5. Respectively, John Merrifield, "An Education Freedom Index: Why, Key Determinants, Component Weights, and Trade-offs," *Journal of School Choice* 5, no. 3 (2011): 319–49; and Andrew J. Coulson, "The Cato Education Market Index," Cato Policy Analysis no. 585, December 13, 2006.

6. Coulson, "The Cato Education Market Index," p. 6.

7. Merrifield, "An Education Freedom Index: Why, Key Determinants, Component Weights, and Trade-offs."

8. Merrifield, "Education Freedom Index."

Chapter 8

1. Randi Weingarten, "Donald Trump vs. Public Schools: Betsy DeVos Is a Radical Choice," *New York Daily News*, December 1, 2016.

2. Benjamin R. Barber, "Public Schooling: Education for Democracy," in *The Public Purpose of Education and Schooling*, ed. John I. Goodlad and Timothy J. McMannon (San Francisco, CA: Jossey-Bass, 1997), p. 22.

3. Benjamin Rush, "Thoughts upon the Mode of Education Proper in a Republic," in *Essays on Education in the Early Republic*, ed. Frederick Rudolph (Cambridge, MA: The Belknap Press of Harvard University Press, 1965), p. 9.

4. Horace Mann, "First Annual Report," in *Lectures, and Annual Reports, on Education*, ed. Mary Mann (Boston: Lee and Shepard, 1872), pp. 417–18.

5. Terry M. Moe, *Schools, Vouchers, and the American Public* (Washington: Brookings Institution Press, 2001), pp. 86–91.

6. Andrew J. Coulson, *Market Education: The Unknown History* (New Brunswick, NJ: Social Philosophy and Policy Center and Transaction Publishers, 1999), p. 85.

7. Andrew Coulson highlighted many conflicts in *Market Education*, and the Cato Institute maintains a growing database of roughly 1,600 modern conflicts that can be searched using Cato's Public Schooling Battle Map.

8. Diane Ravitch, *The Language Police: How Pressure Groups Restrict What Students Learn* (New York: Alfred A. Knopf, 2003); and Michael Berkman and Eric Plutzer, *Evolution, Creationism, and the Battle to Control America's Classrooms* (New York: Cambridge University Press, 2010).

9. Benjamin Justice, *The War That Wasn't: Religious Conflict and Compromise in the Common Schools of New York State, 1865–1900* (Albany, NY: State University of New York Press, 2005).

10. Coulson, *Market Education*, pp. 76–78.

11. Coulson, *Market Education*, pp. 319–20.

12. See, for instance, Diane Ravitch, *The Death and Life of the Great American School System: How Testing and Choice Are Undermining Education*, (New York: Basic Books, 2010); Amy Gutmann, *Democratic Education* (Princeton, NJ: Princeton Paperbacks, 1999); and David Tyack, *Seeking Common Ground: Public Schools in a Diverse Society* (Cambridge, MA: Harvard University Press, 2003).

13. For more on the importance of allowing immigrants to ease into American culture, see Milton M. Gordon, *Assimilation in American Life: The Role of Race, Religion, and National Origin* (New York: Oxford University Press, 1964).

14. David Tyack discusses this, with compelling examples, in *The One Best System: A History of American Urban Education* (Cambridge, MA: Harvard University Press, 1974).

15. "Virginia Statute for Religious Freedom," Thomas Jefferson Foundation website.

16. Andrew J. Coulson, "Forging Consensus: Can the School Choice Community Come Together on an Explicit Goal and a Plan for Achieving It?" Mackinac Center for Public Policy, April 2004.

17. EdChoice, *The ABCs of School Choice: 2016 Edition* (Indianapolis, IN: Friedman Foundation for Educational Choice, 2016).

18. Andrew J. Coulson, "Do Vouchers and Tax Credits Increase Private School Regulation?" *Journal of School Choice* 5, no. 2 (2011): 1–29.

19. Jason Bedrick, Jonathan Butcher, and Clint Bolick, "Taking Credit for Education: How to Fund Education Savings Accounts through Tax Credits," Cato Policy Analysis No. 785, January 20, 2016.

Index

NOTE: Page numbers with letter n indicate notes.

Cato Institute

Founded in 1977, the Cato Institute is a public policy research foundation dedicated to broadening the parameters of policy debate to allow consideration of more options that are consistent with the principles of limited government, individual liberty, and peace. To that end, the Institute strives to achieve greater involvement of the intelligent, concerned lay public in questions of policy and the proper role of government.

The Institute is named for Cato's Letters, libertarian pamphlets that were widely read in the American Colonies in the early 18th century and played a major role in laying the philosophical foundation for the American Revolution.

Despite the achievement of the nation's Founders, today virtually no aspect of life is free from government encroachment. A pervasive intolerance for individual rights is shown by government's arbitrary intrusions into private economic transactions and its disregard for civil liberties. And while freedom around the globe has notably increased in the past several decades, many countries have moved in the opposite direction, and most governments still do not respect or safeguard the wide range of civil and economic liberties.

To address those issues, the Cato Institute undertakes an extensive publications program on the complete spectrum of policy issues. Books, monographs, and shorter studies are commissioned to examine the federal budget, Social Security, regulation, military spending, international trade, and myriad other issues. Major policy conferences are held throughout the year, from which papers are published thrice yearly in the *Cato Journal*. The Institute also publishes the quarterly magazine *Regulation*.

In order to maintain its independence, the Cato Institute accepts no government funding. Contributions are received from foundations, corporations, and individuals, and other revenue is generated from the sale of publications. The Institute is a nonprofit, tax-exempt, educational foundation under Section 501(c)3 of the Internal Revenue Code.

Cato Institute
1000 Massachusetts Ave., N.W.
Washington, D.C. 20001
www.cato.org

www.ingramcontent.com/pod-product-compliance
Lightning Source LLC
Chambersburg PA
CBHW031624040426
42452CB00007B/656